81

Challenges *Smart* Managers Face

HOW TO OVERCOME THE BIGGEST CHALLENGES FACING MANAGERS & LEADERS TODAY

TIM CONNOR, CSP

SOURCEBOOKS INC.
NAPERVILLE, ILLINOIS

Published by Sourcebooks, Inc.
P.O. Box 4410, Naperville, Illinois 60567-4410
(630) 961-3900
Fax: (630) 961-2168
www.sourcebooks.com

Library of Congress Cataloging-in-Publication Data

Connor, Tim
  81 challenges smart managers face : how to overcome the biggest challenges facing managers and leaders today / Tim Connor.
     p. cm.
  Includes index.
  ISBN-13: 978-1-4022-0902-4
  ISBN-10: 1-4022-0902-9
  1. Personnel management. 2. Management. I. Title. II. Title: Eighty-one challenges smart managers face.

HF5549.C7192 2007
658.4—dc22

                                                2006037109

Printed and bound in the United States of America.
VP 10 9 8 7 6 5 4 3 2 1

The man who doesn't read good books has no advantage over the man who can't read them.

—MARK TWAIN

A FEW BESTSELLING BOOKS BY TIM CONNOR

52 Tips for Success, Wealth, and Happiness
How to Be Happy and *Successful from A–Z*
How to Sell More in Less Time
Life Questions
Nitpickers, Naggers, and Tyrants
OK, God, What's Next?
Peace of Mind
Sales Mastery
Soft Sell
That's Life! 41 Life Challenges and How to Handle Them
The Ancient Scrolls
The Last Goodbye
The Male Gift-Giving Survival Guide
The Road to Happiness Is Full of Potholes
The Sales Handbook
The Trade-Off
The Voyage
Your First Year in Sales

To each of my clients over the years who have contributed to my knowledge, experience, and understanding: a special Thank You.

CONTENTS

PREFACE

Why another book on management? If you check Amazon or your local bookstore, you will find hundreds, if not thousands, of books on every aspect of management, leadership, supervision, and related topics written during the past fifty-plus years. So, why one more book on this overworked subject?

I could tell you any number of possible reasons, but the primary one is this: I have read most of the current books on these topics, and although many of them are good and a few are worthy of my praise, most of them fail to address the critical issues and challenges facing managers today. And when managers do not deal successfully with these routine challenges, whether small or significant, it costs their organizations market share, customer loyalty, employee performance, and profits.

This book specifically addresses the thirteen major areas of challenge. The format is simple, the ideas are straightforward, and the objective is clear: to help you identify those challenges that you or members of your management team are facing that may be affecting your bottom line and to give you practical and inexpensive suggestions to handle these challenges once and for all.

Having said this, I don't mean to imply that this will be easy. There will be change and work required of you if you are to reap short- and long-term benefits. It takes courage and commitment to become what I call a "leading-edge" manager, business owner, or executive.

There is one major premise woven through each of the topics covered: if you have a problem, crisis, issue, or any negative situation in your business, department, division, or group, look up the ladder for the cause and down the ladder for the solution. If you are a manager with a tendency to reverse this process, you have a great deal to gain from this book.

Obviously, managers face more than 81 challenges. But most of the ones not covered are addressed either directly or indirectly in the 81 that are included.

The most critical section of this book, "It's Your Turn," comes toward the end of the book. The workbook format of this section will help you identify and put into operation the changes you need to make in your management, communication, or leadership style in order to become a leading-edge manager.

Of course, you can always benefit from reading just a chapter here or there. You may even have a number of "Aha!" experiences. But transformation requires more than this. It requires self-awareness, a willingness to change, a plan to implement, and a follow-up strategy to ensure on-going success.

Completing the workbook section is essential to getting this material out of your head and into action, transforming your management behavior and your organization.

So reading is not enough. Mastery requires study and personalization of the concepts, techniques, and ideas learned. My work is done: I wrote the book. Your work will begin after you have read it.

Self-reverence, self-knowledge,
self-control—these three alone
lead to success.

—ALFRED LORD TENNYSON

INTRODUCTION

Management is a science, an art, and a calling. It requires the patience of Job, the dedication of an Olympic athlete, the persistence of a child, the people skills of a loving grandparent, the study-focus of Einstein, and the humorous outlook of George Burns.

In my book *91 Mistakes Smart Salespeople Make*, I share a simple concept that is appropriate for this book as well. That concept states that there are only three ways to improve your management outcomes and results: Do more right. Do less wrong. Or do both. In this book I will share numerous ideas, techniques, and concepts that, when understood, embraced, and followed, will have a positive impact on your management style and outcomes.

One of the critical factors for success in management is a healthy and positive self-image. Essentially a person's self-image will determine:

- How they feel about themselves and others
- How they view the world around them
- How they respond to life's circumstances
- How they determine what goals to set for themselves
- How they react to failure and adversity

- How they behave when no one is looking
- How they handle difficult situations
- How they envision their own destiny

Organizations are made up of groups of individuals with various self-images that together create an "organizational self-image." Organizations also create a destiny, which is often consistent with how the combined group of employees in a department, division, group, or even the entire organization see themselves as an entity. For example, if employees in a customer service department see themselves as unimportant and unappreciated, the department will typically treat customers in much the same way. Yes, there may be select individuals who treat customers with respect and concern. But generally speaking, because of its low self-image, the department will treat most customers poorly.

If the management team in an organization is not in sync with its direction, goals, decisions, strategy, philosophy, and communication, it will create confusion, lack of harmony, under-empowered employees, and poor employee performance. If the members of a sales team feel that they are unnecessary, are constantly under pressure to perform, receive little or no positive reinforcement or appreciation, or feel that other departments or senior management perceives them only as arrogant troublemakers, their individual self-image will become the "group self-image." The results of this "corporate self-image" are often the same as in the list of consequences mentioned previously. One common sales outcome of poor self-image is to meet price resistance by generally reducing price rather than selling value, thereby contributing to low margins and profits.

Are management roles changing? In today's business environment, a number of conditions are impacting the roles of managers today. A few of them include the following:

- Cultural and age diversity
- Impact and use of technology
- A growing international marketplace
- Unclear or inconsistent ethical standards
- Employee stress levels increasing
- Corporate direction and strategy under fire by consumers
- Employee desire for greater independence and autonomy
- Wide range of consumer choices for products and services
- Employees with less-specific skills
- Relentless and accelerating change

Given these factors, I ask you again: are the roles of managers, supervisors, executives, and business owners changing today? Yes! Here are just a few of the areas of change that I have observed during the past several years of coaching and consulting with my clients in various industries worldwide:

- Increased responsibility for large numbers of remote employees
- More time "doing" than "managing"
- Increased time coaching employees on personal issues
- Greater numbers of job openings that can't be filled

- More time communicating via email than in person or by phone
- Less time for their own personal development

Again, I could have included many more, but the essence is this: if you are still using management techniques and behaviors that you used more than five years ago, I guarantee you that you are going to be less effective as a leader, coach, and manager in today's changing world.

But some of the fundamental managerial roles, attitudes, and responsibilities have not changed, such as:
- The need to trust your employees and have your employees trust you
- The need to respect employees' uniqueness
- The need to communicate openly and honestly with employees
- The need to give employees the recognition and appreciation they deserve
- The need to have a clear future career path available to employees
- The need to compensate employees fairly

Read on to learn and unlearn. Read to grow, and read to self-discover.

MANAGEMENT QUIZ

1. You should always praise employees in

   _____.

   A. Private
   B. Public

2. Listening is the most important management skill.
   A. True
   B. False

3. Most managers spend too little time planning.
   A. True
   B. False

4. You should always discipline employees in

   _____.

   A. Private
   B. Public

5. Every employee can benefit from additional training.
   A. True
   B. False

6. Corporate culture should flow _____.
   A. Top-down
   B. Bottom-up

7. Morale is directly related to _____.
   - A. Corporate culture
   - B. Communication patterns
   - C. Stress levels
   - D. Management style
   - E. All of the above

8. Employee's perceptions become _____.
   - A. A nuisance
   - B. Reality

9. One of the biggest managerial weaknesses is failure to give timely positive and negative feedback.
   - A. True
   - B. False

10. Organization direction is one of the biggest employee _____.
    - A. Issues
    - B. Concerns
    - C. Frustrations
    - D. Needs
    - E. All of the above

11. Money and/or benefits are the number one issue with most employees.
    - A. True
    - B. False

12. Most employees feel they receive adequate recognition.
    A. True
    B. False

13. When you hire under pressure you always hire

    _____.

    A. Beneath your standards
    B. The best person for the job

14. One of the major responsibilities of a manager is to motivate their employees.
    A. True
    B. False

15. One of the biggest employee concerns is management

    _____.

    A. Direction
    B. Vacation policy

16. Turnover is the direct result of _____.
    A. Poor hiring
    B. Poor training
    C. Poor compensation plans
    D. Morale
    E. All of the above

17. The best employees come in early and stay late.
    A. True
    B. False

18. Disagreement from an employee is _____.
    A. Positive
    B. Negative
    C. Can be both—and it depends

19. You can't motivate anyone.
    A. True
    B. False

20. Managers do not contribute to employee performance.
    A. True
    B. False

21. Most employees don't care about the organization's success.
    A. True
    B. False

22. Always inspect what you _____.
    A. Purchase
    B. Expect
    C. Delegate

23. You should solicit employee feedback on all issues.
    A. True
    B. False

24. You get the behavior you _____.
    A. Deserve
    B. Reward
    C. Model

25. Good managers hire weaker candidates.
    A. True
    B. False

26. You should only seek opinions that reinforce your opinions.
    A. True
    B. False

27. Keeping a poor employee around _____.
    A. Gives him/her another chance, sending the right message to other employees
    B. Is a sign of management weakness, sending the wrong message to other employees

28. The purpose of negative feedback is to _____.
    A. Change or modify behavior
    B. Aggravate the person/situation being criticized

29. You should always hire attitudes rather than _____.
    A. Skills
    B. Work history

30. You should delegate _____.
    A. Responsibility and authority
    B. Set-up and clean-up duties

31. Most managers are good interviewers.
    A. True
    B. False

32. Organizational goals should be communicated to employees.
    A. True
    B. False

33. A vision statement is _____.
    A. Who you are, who your customers are, how you serve them, and the business you are in
    B. A statement of direction, purpose, and meaning

34. A mission statement is _____.
    A. Who you are, who your customers are, how you serve them, and the business you are in
    B. A statement of direction, purpose, and meaning

35. Family members make good employees.
    A. True
    B. False
    C. It depends

36. Employees like to feel included on things because
_____.
   A. It makes them feel important
   B. It builds trust and respect
   C. They want to feel they belong to something bigger than themselves
   D. They want to take over

37. You should always consult employees when you make decisions that impact them.
   A. True
   B. False

38. You can manage your organization from behind your desk.
   A. True
   B. False

39. Always delegate activities rather than results.
   A. True
   B. False

40. Rules and policies should be flexible.
   A. True
   B. False

41. By not clearly communicating expectations to an employee, you _____.
    A. Improve their performance
    B. Diminish their performance

42. It is important to really know your people.
    A. True
    B. False

43. A lack of empowered employees contributes to _____.
    A. Employee apathy
    B. Poor performance
    C. Lack of trust
    D. Lack of respect
    E. All of the above

44. Having an open-door policy always encourages employees to share issues.
    A. True
    B. False

45. Employees generally want more training.
    A. True
    B. False

46. Politics in an organization is inevitable.
    A. True
    B. False

47. It is impossible to eliminate rumor and hearsay.
    A. True
    B. False

48. Arrogance and ignorance are two of the biggest reasons why organizations fail.
    A. True
    B. False

49. As a manager, you should always _____.
    A. Give the credit and take the responsibility
    B. Give the responsibility and take the credit

50. When you promote your best employee, you will always end up with a good manager.
    A. True
    B. False

Answers are located on page 261.

Your work may be finished someday, but your education, never.

—ALEXANDER DUMAS

Chapter One: *Attitude Challenges*

Chapter Two: *Self-Management Challenges*

Chapter Three: *Planning Challenges*

Chapter Four: *Hiring Challenges*

Chapter Five: *Delegating Challenges*

Chapter Six: *Feedback Challenges*

Chapter Seven: *Motivation Challenges*

40. Motivating Employees
41. Setting a Clear Direction and Focus
42. Empowering Employees
43. Fostering a Fun and Rewarding Culture and Environment
44. Holding People Accountable
45. Rewarding the Right Behavior
46. Maintaining a *What* instead of a *Who* Corporate Culture
47. Being an Encourager
48. Creating a Motivating Climate and Culture
49. Rewarding Performance rather than Tenure or Position
50. Maintaining a Safe Corporate Culture
51. Getting Ownership to Projects and Goals

Chapter Eight: *Coaching Challenges*

52. Playing Fair at Checkers
53. Having and Maintaining Consistent Standards

Chapter Nine: *Training Challenges*

54. Investing in Employee Development
55. Seeing Training as an Investment rather than a Cost
56. Using Outside Resources for Training
57. Developing Curriculum-Based Training
58. Inspecting the Training for Positive Outcomes

Chapter Ten: *Leadership Challenges*

59. Defining and Personalizing Your Leadership Style
60. Making Consistently Good Decisions
61. Sharing the Wealth

CHAPTER 1

ATTITUDE CHALLENGES

I have met hundreds of managers worldwide who were not aware of the impact of their attitudes, philosophy, and life outlook on the performance of their employees and their organization. Many of these managers believed that they managed in a vacuum, oblivious to the ripple effect of the subtle signals they sent throughout their departments day in and day out. Others clearly understood that their every decision or lack of decision, action or inaction, and behaviors were carefully scrutinized by their employees and that it was incumbent upon them to monitor, self-inspect, and self-analyze their attitudes and behaviors on a routine basis.

It is vital that managers stay in touch with their own prejudices, judgments, opinions, management style, and communication patterns. Each of these is an outgrowth of their personality.

Personality is how people behave. These behaviors are generally the result of feelings. If you feel frustrated, you will tend to act frustrated. Feel happy? You'll act happy, and so on. Feelings are driven by attitudes. Attitudes are consistent ways of thinking or feeling about things or people. We create physical and mental habits; these mental habits create habitual ways of thinking or feeling. For example, if you are a bigot, you have most likely formed certain mental habits about certain races, groups, or classes of people. These habits contribute to your attitudes and thus drive your actions or behavior toward people in that group.

Most of our habits are the result of early upbringing and environmental conditioning by society and caregivers. Most psychologists agree that by age ten at the latest, your attitudes about yourself, the world, people, and circumstances are pretty much established. You can change your attitudes, but it takes an awareness that they need to be changed, a desire to change them, patience, time, effort, commitment, and action. None of these are easy, given the tremendous number of things that any person, and particularly a manager, has on his or her plate at any given time.

But it's quite simple, really. If you want to change your outcomes, change your attitudes.

CHALLENGE #1: *Controlling Your Ego*

One of the biggest contributors to poor management performance, bad decisions, hiring mistakes, and a host of other problems is ego. Everyone has an ego. It is a natural part of everyone's psyche and vital for success. The ego wants to look good, be right, not make mistakes, not admit failure, manipulate, and to be in control or appear to be in control at all times. Problems occur though when managers' egos are given too much control over their behaviors, attitudes, and management styles.

What I have discovered is that not only do individuals have an ego, but many organizations also function as if there was an "organization ego." I know Freud would have a problem with this concept, but I have seen too many organizations fail or do poorly purely as a result of—not the ego of an individual—but an underlying ego force that resonates from the organization as a whole.

It would be nice if organizations and their strategies, objectives, goals, purpose, mission, and performance were always predictable and operating at peak efficiency and optimum results. However, in the real world, change is the norm. Uncertainty prevails. And there are forces at work that would sabotage your ideal world. They include: unpredictable employees, technology, competitors, customer attitudes and expectations, the government, and the weather, just to mention a few. If all of these could be harnessed for optimum control, we would never have business failures, lost customers, unhappy or poorly performing employees, disgruntled suppliers, or frustrated accountants.

Businesspeople's uncontrolled egos have cost Corporate America more money than any other single factor. Uncontrolled egos have resulted in poor decisions, thwarted initiatives, the failure of products that have outlived their life cycle, and acquisitions gone bad. Want more?

- New products that should never have hit the street
- Bad products that were left on the street too long
- Poor hiring decisions
- The termination of good employees for no other reason than that they have egos too
- The unwillingness to let go of the control of anything
- Keeping decision-making at the top of the corporate ladder
- Unwillingness to delegate difficult or critical tasks
- The desire to look good to the rest of the corporate world, regardless of whether you are making money or not

I believe by now I should have your attention. So why is ego such a big problem in business? After all, Donald Trump has one, and he is successful.

If you were to ask an executive or manager with an out-of-control-ego if his or her ego is out of control, guess what you will hear? Believe it or not: no. Why is this? Denial? Arrogance? Insecurity? Or is there some other psychological or emotional need that is not being met?

During my career, I have watched clients make acquisitions (against my recommendations) for no other reason than ego. In almost every case, their decisions cost their organization dearly in focus and reputation, not to mention profits. Ultimately, many of these companies were shut down or sold off to some *other* executive with a big ego, maybe this time to someone who prides him- or herself as being a business savior or turn-around master!

Before I lose you, I don't want you to get the impression that ego is only an issue in the big decisions or choices made at the top. Its impact can be found day-to-day in many of the small and often less significant parts of an enterprise—in the actions and decisions made by mid-level managers and supervisors. I see the results of ego every day and everywhere I go in my travels as a speaker and trainer.

As a manager, how do you know if your ego is out of control? Just pay close attention to a number of critical factors. I guarantee that if you are aware of your circumstances, honest with your self-appraisal, and in touch with reality, it will become crystal clear whether your ego is adequately in check or running rampant in your organization or department. Some of the factors indicating problems with an out-of-control ego are:

- Consistently poor morale
- Constant communication breakdowns
- Bad hiring decisions
- Consistently poor decisions
- Acquisitions or mergers that go sour
- High employee turnover
- Consistently poor quality
- Outdated policies, products, services, and/or procedures
- Loss of market share
- Vulnerability to competitors
- Poor sales results
- Decreasing profits from year to year

Carefully observe early warning signs for these factors and determine their cause and any relationship between them and your ego, and then respond to them and manage them effectively and without ego before they become embedded in your corporate culture, employee attitudes, and customer attitudes.

Ask yourself:

1. Can I ever be wrong?
2. Can an employee be smarter than I am?
3. Do I trust my employees?
4. Can I reverse myself after a bad decision, or do I die by it?
5. Can I give up control?
6. Do I have pet projects or activities that I can't let go of?
7. Can I freely give credit where someone else was responsible for the positive outcome?
8. Can I discard old products, services, or ideas that I was responsible for?
9. Can I share the limelight with others?
10. Do I give adequate appreciation and recognition to others?
11. Can I admit failure?
12. Can I admit to not having an answer?
13. Do I procrastinate on simple or important tasks, decisions, or initiatives?

These questions should get you started. Honest answers will help you clearly identify if your ego is a problem in your position.

In his classic book *Good to Great: Why Some Companies Make the Leap...and Others Don't*, Jim Collins states: "Level 5 leaders channel their ego needs away from themselves and into the larger goal of building a great company. It's not that Level 5 leaders have no ego or self-interest. Indeed they are incredibly ambitious—but their ambition is first and foremost for their institution and not her or himself."

If you can rise to the challenge of channeling your ego in this way, be encouraged by the following:

1. Your ego is not part of your DNA or genes. It is man-made and can be unmade or controlled if you choose.
2. It is better to succeed and enjoy your success with a controlled ego than it is to go down in flames with an ego that is out of control.
3. You will never "win them all," no matter how good you think you are. So get used to losing once in a while, if you haven't already.
4. Hire a personal coach. The cost will be peanuts compared with the time and money you could save your organization. I accept ten new coaching clients every year. If you want to be considered for one of the slots, give me a call.
5. Business is not about winning or looking good, but serving others well.

I believe the first test of a really great man is his humility.

—JOHN RUSKIN

CHALLENGE #2: *Being Responsible* to *Employees rather than* for *Them*

Although you are responsible for your employees' output, productivity, and results, you are responsible *to* people, not *for* them. Some individuals mistakenly think that being responsible for people is the same as having sympathy for them. Sympathy keeps people dependent. You feel that if they fail, you have failed. Being responsible to people requires empathy: you understand what they are going through, but it is their stuff, not yours. You are there to help them, support them, and give them the tools and training they need to be effective. But if they fail to perform, it is clearly their choice. (Of course, if you haven't done what is required of you, then you should feel responsible for them.)

How can managers be responsible to their employees rather than for them?

1. Make no excuses for poor employee performance.
2. Apply empathy when employees have personal issues that may get in the way of their effectiveness.
3. Permit no negative attitudes from top performers.
4. Permit no employees to break the rules that others must follow.
5. Don't play favorites with certain employees.

Personal responsibility is an absolute requirement if employees are to succeed and contribute their share to the overall success of your department or organization. Tolerating less than the acceptable standards from certain employees, for whatever reason, sends a message to other employees that the rules and expectations vary, depending on who you are, your age, gender, race, experience, personal challenges, tenure, performance, or relationship with the manager.

Everything you do as a manager sends subtle signals to everyone. Be vigilant to ensure that the signals you are sending are uniform and consistent. Sure, there may be situations when exceptions can and should be made, due to personal issues or challenges. Just be careful that these don't set precedents that you are unwilling to apply across the entire organization.

CHALLENGE #3: *Treating Employees the Same, Yet Differently*

Treating individuals the same, yet differently, at first glance might seem to contradict the previous one we just discussed. But read on and carefully observe, and you will see some very subtle differences.

All employees have special needs and desires that are uniquely theirs. They have dreams and hopes and the desire to feel valuable. Some may express them openly, while others may keep them hidden in the safety zone of their own minds. Or they may communicate them to their peers rather than to their supervisors. But each employee is uniquely individual.

Treating employees without regard for these personal needs sends a clear message that they are not special and are just another cog in the machine. If you want the labor of a person's heart and not just their hands or mind, it is critical that you treat people with respect. This is seemingly a simple task, but you would be amazed at how frequently managers show disrespect for their employees in both subtle and blatant ways. Some managers:

- Discipline an employee in front of their peers.
- Interrupt them while they are sharing an idea or solution to a problem.
- Arrive late for a meeting with an employee.
- Fail to copy them in correspondence or emails that impact their position.
- Ignore or dismiss their suggestions.
- Fail to listen to them.

It is impossible to know every employee's needs and desires from moment to moment. But you can learn to see every employee as special and unique. This takes time, the willingness to let go of prejudices and judgments, and the ability to learn to see all employees as a valuable contributors to the organization's success, well-being, and future growth—and to invest in them accordingly.

CHALLENGE #4: *Letting Go of Prejudices and Judgments*

Since holding on to prejudices and judgments can seriously undermine your effectiveness as a manager, your challenge is to let go of them. Prejudices can take many forms but generally are the result of your expectations, personal philosophy, experiences, life outlook, and personal agendas.

Remember that when you judge another person, it says more about who you are than who they are. Most judgments and prejudices are the result of your personal perceptions.

No one looks at life—its events, conditions, or circumstances—in the same way. We see life not as it is, but as we perceive it. Each of us has a mental filter through which we interpret events, circumstances, and other people's behavior. Ten people can look at the same new product, marketing piece, decision, sales objective, policy, or procedure and see it differently. This gives life its diversity and gives relationships their challenges.

Business relationships are no exception. Take faults, for instance. Do you know someone who has faults? Be honest now. Look closely at them for a moment. Aren't another person's faults what that person thinks, feels, believes, or does differently than what you think they should feel, think, believe, or act? The assumption you are making when you maintain that another person has a fault is that your way of feeling or acting is either better than theirs or right while theirs is wrong.

But there is no right or wrong way for an individual to think, feel, or believe. Everyone is unique. In interpersonal relationships, the need to change the other person to your way of thinking because you believe theirs is wrong and yours is right is one of the biggest issues that cause stress and conflict. Acceptance is one of the biggest hurdles people face in relationships, whether personal or professional.

Learning to accept others' differences is also a major issue when it comes to motivating ourselves on a consistent basis. If you fail to perceive life and its events and people clearly, you will tend to fall into any number of demotivating traps such as guilt, blame, resentment, anger, and other negative emotions or feelings. These negative responses will color your use of talent and how you treat others on a regular basis.

What if an employee believes that he is underpaid? What if a customer believes she has been treated poorly? What if a stockholder believes you have acted unwisely? All of these are perceptions in their minds. Are they true or false? It doesn't matter. If they believe them, then they are true for them.

Where do prejudices and judgments cloud your view of life, people, work, events, and circumstances? How do they affect you now? Have prejudices and judgments had a negative impact on your life in the past, and is it possible they will affect you in the future? Where do you need a clearer vision and more accurate perceptual integrity?

Only in growth, reform, and change, paradoxically enough, is true security found.

—ANNE MORROW LINDBERGH

CHALLENGE #5: *Making Yourself Truly Indispensable*

It is common for people to want to be considered indispensable in their jobs. After all, the competition is out there; the certain generations or groups are more numerous and demanding. The challenge for employees today is to constantly build your value to your organization through personal integrity, humility, and creativity.

Look at the more common picture. Managers who feel they are indispensable often behave in ways that are contrary to their organization's success. Their goals, decisions, actions, and personality styles seem to communicate that no one can manage the roles and responsibilities of their department better then they can. They feel that without them, their organization or department would fail miserably. This is an example of an individual with an out-of-control ego who is arrogant, ignorant, or a combination of these factors. Such behavior can also be caused by poor self-image or insecurity.

People who feel they are indispensable to the company tend to exhibit a "my way or the highway" style of management. The impact of a manager with this outlook isn't a pretty picture. To believe you are indispensable is totally naive. If this "lone giant" attitude is a part of your psyche, I recommend you consider the following:

1. How was your department or organization able to function before you arrived?
2. When you take a week off for vacation, does everything fall apart at the seams?
3. Are you cultivating employees to take on additional

roles or responsibilities that are part of your job function?

4. Do you tend to delegate only unimportant or inconsequential work to your employees?

Smart managers or leaders, though, who truly make themselves indispensable, will constantly build their value by staying on top of their game and enlarging their vision of the future. To do this, they will:

1. Offer employees adequate training.
2. Hire strong candidates so the employees will contribute to the good of the department and company.
3. Delegate tasks or assignments to help employees grow in skills and responsibilities.

Make yourself indispensable and you'll be moved up. Act as if you are indispensable and you'll be moved out.

—ANONYMOUS

CHALLENGE #6: *Knowing You Need to Keep Improving*

It should be clear by now that if you think you are as good as you need to be, you need to think again. Let's start with three key questions:

1. Are you spending time consistently improving your management and people skills?
2. What have you invested so far this year in your own personal and career development?
3. What is your working philosophy of routinely investing time and resources in your personal and career development?

I am often amazed at how many managers are quick to send their employees to seminars and skill-development programs while they sit in their offices trying to figure out why sales are down, performance is marginal, profits are lagging, and organizational effectiveness is nearly chaotic. If you have never attended my two-day management boot camp, let me share one of the critical premises from this program: everything in your organization is a "top-down" issue.

1. If top-down communication is ineffective, bottom-up communication will be poor.
2. If top-down direction is unclear or confusing, bottom-up performance will be deficient.
3. If top-down trust is absent, bottom-up trust will be negligible.
4. If top-down ownership of projects or initiatives is inconsistent, bottom-up actions will be timid.

5. If top-down leadership is lacking, bottom-up effectiveness will be missing.
6. If top-down messages are mixed, bottom-up morale will be inconsistent.
7. If top-down decision-making is tentative, bottom-up performance will falter.

Is this enough incentive to keep improving yourself? As I've said before: if you have a problem in your organization, look up the ladder for the cause and down the ladder for the solution. Unfortunately, many organizations today act in the reverse. They look down for the cause and up for the solution.

To assure organizational excellence, the solution is for managers to develop a game plan for their own ongoing self-development. There are many ways to achieve this:

1. Hire a career or business coach.
2. Attend management classes on a routine basis.
3. Attend at least one personal development seminar or program per month.
4. Join a business Book-of-the-Month Club.
5. Listen to audio programs on business areas that interest you and will benefit you.
6. Obtain a business mentor.
7. Attend a management forum.
8. Bring a professional trainer into your organization to conduct a custom management or leadership program.
9. Get active in your industry's association.
10. Attend networking events in your industry or at your professional level.

11. Join a professional organization such as the CEO Clubs, Young Presidents' Organization, or Executive Committee.

If you are investing in your employees' development so they can be better equipped to more effectively perform their jobs as the world changes, don't you think it would make sense for you to do the same for yourself? Why not try a simple rule of thumb: for every dollar and hour you invest in your employees' development as a group, invest 10 percent of both in your own development.

You can never ride on the wave that came in and went out yesterday.

—JOHN WANAMAKER

CHALLENGE #7: *Working with a Coach or Mentor*

Operating in a vacuum simply doesn't work. You can't learn everything you need to learn to be an effective manager on your own. Successful managers understand the importance of working with a mentor, a coach, or role model to help them as they move through their careers. Managers who believe they don't need this type of help or can't benefit from the counsel, feedback, suggestions, ideas, or help of someone who has "been there" and who can pass along their experiences are seriously sabotaging their ability to achieve greatness as a manager and leader.

Having a mentor or coach can shave years off the learning curve in your career. It is essential to interact with people who are where you want to be or with people who have done what you want to do. The key is to create a win-win relationship with them. Working with a mentor or a coach is one of the many ways to accomplish this objective.

Who is a mentor or a coach? He is a person who is interested in your success, happiness, well-being, or future, and wants to help you succeed. These people don't necessarily have to be in the same business, have the same interests, or even have been successful in their chosen field. What a mentor or coach does need to have and bring to the relationship is insight, integrity, a willingness to help, genuine concern, and accountability to you and the ability to provide you with feedback.

You don't need hundreds of mentors or coaches. One can accelerate your career, two can skyrocket it, and three can keep you learning and growing nonstop.

I suggest you look through your contacts to see if you can find someone who can contribute to your career success, and ask him or her to help you. Even if the person is a thousand miles away, you can have a telephone coaching or mentoring relationship.

The key to a successful mentor or coaching relationship is setting the ground rules up front as to each person's roles, expectations, agendas, time use, accountability, and feedback. The right mentor or coach can save you time, energy, and money. He or she can challenge your thinking, hold you accountable, and help you reach your goals. You can even have fun in the process.

You get the best effort from others not by lighting a fire beneath them, but by building a fire within.

—BOB NELSON

CHAPTER 2

SELF-MANAGEMENT CHALLENGES

It is well said that the only limitations we encounter in life are those we place on ourselves. If this is true, why do so few people reach their full potential? Why do so many people feel stuck, out of control, and hopeless in their lives?

Why do so many people give up, quit, settle, resign themselves, or operate out of blame, anger, guilt, resentment, and self-pity when it comes to the quality of their life or their work? People who do not want to take responsibility for their lives insist on pointing their finger toward something or someone else for the cause of their circumstances.

I have been at the bottom of the barrel a few times in my life. I have also reached the mountaintop. In my travels as a speaker, I have met thousands of people who believe they do not have any choices. They are stuck: stuck in a job, business, relationship, and way of life, neighborhood, climate, or career. But you and I are not trees. We can move. We can change what we do not like. Why don't we? Typically, people do not change because of fear, comfort, procrastination, wrong motives or reasons, and emotional manipulation of us by others—and our acceptance of it.

The truth is, each of us came into this world headed for greatness in some way. We were engineered for success at birth and became conditioned for failure along the way. We have forgotten our heritage. We have in our skulls the most magnificent organ ever created: a mind that can create whatever it chooses. There is nothing we cannot do. We can realize whatever we put our minds to, as long as we put action behind our dreams. Most of us could do more if we would only learn that most of our ceilings are self-imposed.

What inner mental images are you holding in your consciousness that may be holding you back? Is it the fear of failure or success? Is it the fear of rejection or public scorn? Is it an inner feeling of unworthiness? Or is there some other emotional issue that you have failed to recognize or deal with?

Self-management requires a number of effective skills, positive attitudes, and consistent disciplines. Without them, you are doomed to a life of frustration, anxiety, and stress.

Disorganization contributes to people's confusion, lack of focus, and poor results. Whether you manage a group of twenty-five employees in a branch or dozens of executives spread out across the globe, or you are a manager who has direct responsibility only for yourself and your own work, I can tell you from experience that the most effective managers understand the difference between being efficient and being effective.

Being efficient is doing things well or right. Being effective is doing the *right* things well or right. There is a subtle, yet important difference between the two.

How do you know if you are operating efficiently or effectively? There are five simple tests.

1. Do you consistently deal with repetitive problems, challenges, or issues? If you do, it is a sure sign that you are not as effective as you could be.
2. Do you tend to have more on your plate than you can handle proficiently? If you do, you are not acting effectively.
3. Do you have a time management problem? Again, same answer.
4. Are you an effective delegator? If not, same answer.
5. Does your job or career cause you a great deal of stress? If yes, same answer.

There are ways to determine if you are acting effectively, but these five will help you determine if you need to develop systems, strategies, routines, or habits to become more organized and effective.

You enhance other people's lives
as you enhance your own.
—MARSHA SINETAR

CHALLENGE #8: *Relying on Technology while Keeping the Human Touch*

Business involves the human connection between customers, employees, suppliers, investors, and the community. Yet our increasing reliance on technology puts us in jeopardy of losing the human touch altogether in business.

I believe, however, that technology is important. It can accelerate the sales process, improve employee education, and help you keep in touch with remote employees and customers. Since business is about relationships and people serving people, though, it is vital that we not lose our perspective regarding the use of technology—and its costs. One big cost is that if we fail to forge positive and trusting relationships, our businesses will fail.

One of the biggest challenges facing employees today is learning how to use technology as a tool and not a crutch. If you have a choice to send an email, call, or visit an employee whose office is down the hall, the tendency today is to send an email or text message. Why not take the trip down the hall? Sure, it might take a few more minutes, but, in the end, you will be enhancing the relationship in a more positive way than by sending an email. Teleconferences can save time and money, but they do not replace the full sensory communication of body language and the nuances of human interaction gained when several people meet face to face. If you are a sales manager, are you spending adequate time in the field or are you just sitting at your computer sending messages day in and day out?

Technology and all of its applications can help you grow your business quickly and exponentially, but if it is not managed, you may lose good employees and customers and become its victim. If you have ever had your technology break down, you know exactly what I am talking about. Use technology to help you where it is appropriate, but be careful: if it gets in the way of building trusting and loyal relationships, you may pay a heavy price.

Technology shapes society and society shapes technology.

—Robert W. White

CHALLENGE #9: *Focusing on What You Want*

We tend to bring into our life that which is consistent with our focus. You can either focus on what is not working or what is, what you don't have or you do, what you want or what you don't, what you believe in or don't. As the familiar saying goes: "Be careful what you ask for, you might just get it."

One of my favorite quotes is by the late tennis great Arthur Ashe. He said, "True greatness is: Starting where you are, using what you have, and doing what you can." Most winners in life are grateful for their blessings and focus on what they desire, have, and can do. By the same token, most losers focus on what is missing, where they are not, and what they can't do. Let me give you an example.

Manager A focuses on policies that are outdated, procedures that are no longer pertinent, and yesterday's issues or problems. Manager B understands a simple management truth: it is easier to apologize than it is to ask permission. Manager B focuses on getting the job done and the results, while manager A focuses on the process. (I am not suggesting that some of these policies might not need to be changed.) The key here is: do what you can within the framework of what is available to you and get on with it. Whining about what is missing or can't be done keeps you stuck in the past. You have three options in any situation or circumstance: change it, accept it, or leave it.

A key ingredient in all leaders, winners, effective people, and productive and successful organizations is focus. What is your focus today? Is it on what you can do or what you cannot? Or is it on what you have or what you don't?

You cannot dream yourself into a character;
you must hammer and forge yourself one.

—JAMES A. FROUDE

CHALLENGE #10: *Knowing When to Involve Others*

Why do managers do things that their employees easily could be—and often should be—doing as a part of their job requirements? If I have heard it once, I have heard it a thousand times: "By the time I tell my employee what to do, show them how to do it, inspect it after they have done it, and follow through with it, I could have done it myself."

The assumptions many managers are making here are:

1. No one can do it better than I can.
2. No one can do it as well as I can.
3. No one can do it as effectively as I can.
4. No one can do it as fast as I can.

But managers who rise to the challenge of involving others—whether their own employees or those from other departments—can reap many benefits. Some of these benefits include the following:

1. They have time for some of their more important duties, tasks, or projects, especially those that are properly the manager's.
2. They discover that their employees may have better and more effective or resourceful ways of doing things.
3. They contribute to the growth and development of their employees.
4. They can break away from behaviors, decision-making processes, planning styles, or other management roles or responsibilities that may be limiting them as well as

the organization by listening to the new and creative thinking of those around them.

It is amazing how much you can accomplish when it doesn't matter who gets the credit.

—UNKNOWN

CHALLENGE #11: *Setting the Right Example*

How many individuals do you know who say that they manage by example, when, in reality, they don't practice what they preach? And what exactly is managing by example? I have heard the phrase often, yet I believe that many of the people who utter it don't know what it means.

I believe management by example means congruence. A person who manages by example exhibits consistency between their behavior and their expectations of others, their actions towards others, and their beliefs about what is right.

Unfortunately, managers and executives who hold a double standard are everywhere. Watch the nightly news, pick up the morning paper or a business magazine and, I guarantee it, there will be news of another business calamity. Perhaps there will be news of a chief executive officer (CEO), president, or chief financial officer (CFO) charged with some infraction or lapse in integrity. Or there will be reports of another business ethics scandal or a massive discrepancy between executive and employee dollars and perks. This lack of consistency has become more noticeable over the past fifty years.

In contrast to this negative image, thousands of companies in Corporate America are being run by ethical, conservative, generous, and caring executives and entrepreneurs. They go about their daily business serving their employees and customers without public aggravation or agitation.

The challenge is for managers to create a culture of respect, trust, congruence, and integrity—period. Doing this means living by a set of standards that become your mantra, regardless of your mood, economic conditions, or the weather. These standards become the benchmark for acceptable attitudes and behaviors that must relate to everyone in your organization, no matter their position, tenure, performance, gender, age, nationality, or race. When you can say honestly that your behavior is consistent with what you expect from your employees all of the time, you will have mastered this vital challenge.

Quality is not an act. It is a habit.

—ARISTOTLE

CHALLENGE #12: *Having a Consistent Management Style*

Managers today must interact with and supervise employees who vastly differ in age, personality, and other factors that the previous generation of managers never dreamed of. Let's take a brief look at the different types of employees today:

- Baby Boomers (the generation born between the years of 1946 and 1964)
- X- and Y-Generations (generation Xers are people born between 1961 and 1981, and individuals in generation Y were born between 1977 and 2003)
- Graying generation
- People of all ethnicities
- People with different sexual orientations
- Individuals with disabilities
- Women and men
- Teenagers
- Part-timers

If you think you can manage each of these employee categories the same way, think again or consider a new career. Each of these groups has different:

- Perspectives
- Histories
- Outlooks
- Emotional needs
- Personal agendas
- Career objectives
- Lifestyle needs/challenges

- Financial obligations
- Education levels

Face it: you can't manage all employees the same way. If you try, I guarantee that you will experience a great deal of frustration, stress, and sleepless nights. The challenge of being consistent means attending to what these different groups have in common. These people:
- Want you to care
- Want to feel like they belong
- Want to feel a sense of satisfaction from their employee roles
- Want appreciation and recognition
- Want to feel a certain sense of control over their destiny or life
- Want to be treated fairly
- Want to be communicated with
- Want you to listen to them
- Want to be seen as individuals regardless of their membership in any particular group

Success is more a function of consistent common sense than it is of genius.

—An Wang

CHALLENGE #13: *Managing Your Stressors*

Due to the corporate frenzy to restructure, downsize, right-size, reconstruct, or you-name-it, managers everywhere are under greater stress. They face increased expectations to exceed quotas, improve margins, cut costs, improve productivity, and do it all with fewer people, less time, and less money. Add to this bleak outlook the increased pressure from family, friends, and society to do more, spend more time with the family, the dog, and Aunt Sarah, and keep the grass cut and the yard looking like it just came out of *Southern Living* magazine.

No wonder middle managers in record numbers are bailing out of Corporate America and buying franchises, getting into multi-level marketing (MLM), or buying Winnebago recreational vehicles or new golf clubs. At least when you work for yourself—not your boss—you can decide what your stressors are.

But the real stress culprit is not what is going on outside us but what is going on inside. Stress is not caused by an event or person. Stress is your "inside-out" reaction to "outside-in" people, events, or circumstances.

What is your typical reaction to stressful situations? Do you hide, run, get angry, get busy, blame, get emotional, cry, or scream?

If you put two people in the middle of the same problem, they will react differently. One may get all stressed out, while the other stays calm and poised, working through to a solution. The challenge is to learn how to handle and manage your stressors in any of the following ways:

1. Keep reevaluating your goals on a regular basis (at least once a year). Let go of the ones that no longer interest you, then focus on and work toward the ones that do.

2. Keep balance in your life. People who burn out tend to lack harmony in their overall life. They focus on only work or only family.

3. Spend time in reflection and introspection. What is really important at this stage of your life? Let the other stuff go. You can come back to any or all of it at some future time—if you still want to.

4. Develop support systems—people to talk with and listen to who are successfully dealing with similar circumstances.

5. Have more fun. Lighten up. Enjoy each day of life with all its simple, yet wonderful, gifts—air, food, water, color, sounds, sights, smiles, loving relationships, and unexpected kind words from a friend.

Circumstances do not determine a man,
they reveal who he really is.

—JAMES LANE ALLEN

CHALLENGE #14: *Letting Go of Old Emotional Baggage*

What is holding you back and causing you stress? Was it something your parents did twenty years ago? Was it something your boss said last week? Or was it something a spouse or friend said yesterday?

Old baggage can be defined as emotional problems we carry around with us for days, months, or years. It is usually negative stuff like old hurts, resentments, or anger. It can also be some old guilt, failure, or fear that affects our current relationships and life in general.

Why do people hold on to all of these old feelings? For one reason, old baggage can feel very comfortable after a while—so comfortable, as a matter of fact, that many people go to their grave without being able to let go of these hurts, slights, and pain.

There is a very good reason to let go of all of this old baggage. Stress from suppressed emotions that fester in the body take their toll on various aspects of our physiology. For example, old baggage is one of the biggest causes of stress which can kill you if you don't let it go.

I'm told that the way to catch monkeys is to put bunches of bananas in large glass jugs with long narrow necks and then spread them on the ground. A monkey shows up, puts his arm in the jug, grabs the bananas, and then won't let go. He would rather end up in the Bronx Zoo than let go of his bananas. Thousands of psychologists and counselors around the country are getting anywhere from $100 to $300 an hour, and what are they trying to do? You guessed it: help people let go of their bananas.

What do you need to let go of today? What is preventing you from letting it go? What harm is being done to a relationship or your career or business by not letting it go? Accept the challenge and let it go.

It's not what we don't know that hurts;
it's what we know that ain't so.

—WILL ROGERS

CHALLENGE #15: *Getting Out from Behind Your Desk*

You can't manage your organization from behind your desk. You can coach, train, inspect, lead, and direct only when you are in the presence of your employees.

You would be amazed at how many managers hide behind paperwork, meetings, busy schedules, and a variety of avoidance tactics. I guarantee that if you are not visible to your employees on a regular basis, stuff—important stuff—is falling between the cracks.

Being visible allows you to:

- Catch people doing things right, then recognize and appreciate them.
- Catch people doing things wrong, and modify their behavior through coaching.
- Keep in touch with the reality of your department or organization.
- Be available for questions, concerns, or the needs of your employees.
- Find new, creative ways to run your department.
- Be a sounding board for your employees.
- Let your employees know that you care and are interested in them and their jobs.
- Fix things before they break or break down completely
- Break things that need to be broken.
- Determine common perceptions—or misperceptions—that people have about the business, their jobs, or customers.

The most effective managers and leaders today get to know their people. People know their frustrations, concerns, questions, beliefs, problems, dreams, goals, strengths, and weaknesses. You can't know any of this if you are barricaded behind piles of reports, nonstop meetings, and a heavy workload.

CHALLENGE #16: *Maintaining Balance*

I don't care if you are the CEO of a hundred-million-dollar company—it's still just a job. Sure, it's an important one, and many employees and their families rely on you doing your job well, but it's still just a job.

I am amazed at how many managers, executives, and business owners sacrifice their health, families, friends, interests, and peace of mind because of their jobs. Let's face it, folks: I don't care if you started the company, bought it in your forties, inherited it, or got caught in the middle of a merger or acquisition. Either it was there before you got there, or it will be there after you are gone.

In life, you win some and you lose some. You aren't going to win all of your battles or lose them all, so why not just enjoy life, the ride, and your job? Your job or career is just one part of that whole life. Sure, it may be the economic engine that provides for your lifestyle, but is all of that money worth the stress, frustration, lack of inner peace, sacrificed relationships, and lack of fun?

I once worked with a client who was seventy-eight years old and still running his company. He had capable managers and employees who had proven they could run and grow his organization. One day I asked him, "George, why are you still working twelve-hour days, six days a week? Why don't you spend some time enjoying the rest of your life?" He replied, "What else would I do? It's all I know. It's all that is important to me." I wonder if he will have those same answers on his deathbed.

Believe me, I am not advocating retirement. In a recent study, AARP, the not-for-profit organization for older adults in the U.S., said that for those who retire at age sixty-five, the average life span is only five to seven additional years. What I am suggesting is some degree of balance. If George took a few weeks or months off to spend time with his family, to travel, or just relax, I guarantee he wouldn't return to a company that was in shambles. It might even be running better! Who knows? Enjoy your life while you can.

CHAPTER 3

PLANNING CHALLENGES

A lack of effective planning wastes time and corporate resources. It also causes more employee turnover, poor morale, and lack of performance than any other single management role, responsibility, or activity.

Show me companies that are always fighting an uphill battle toward profitable growth, and I will show you companies that plan in hindsight, not at all, or with no routine or strategy in mind. Conversely, organizations that consistently succeed and prosper spend adequate time planning at every level of the organization.

Managers who effectively plan an activity, project, strategy, campaign, or business event can save money, time, and energy and will contribute greatly to their bottom line, competitive position, and overall reputation and success. (Please keep in mind that if there is enough time and money to fix things, make them better, or improve them after they've come apart, then there is time and money enough to do them right the first time.)

To get you started or to give you new ideas, here are some of the areas where managers, business owners, and executives should spend time planning:

- A yearly strategic planning meeting
- A weekly sales/staff meeting
- A national sales/managers' meeting
- A marketing strategy or approach
- A customer or users' conference/seminar
- A new project or initiative
- The introduction of a new product/service to the market
- The introduction of a new policy/procedure

Now consider ten easy planning steps:

1. Set aside a regular time to plan—for example, once a day, week, month, or year—and let nothing interfere with this business activity.
2. Allocate an amount of time that you will devote to each planning session, such as ten minutes once a day, an hour once a week, or a day once a month.
3. Establish an agenda or make a list of outcomes you want to come out of your planning session, for instance, an accurate budget, a new employee profile, a marketing strategy for a new product, or a to-do list of what you want to accomplish today.
4. Consider the short- and long-term ripple effects of every action or decision as a result of your plan.
5. Put some benchmarks, measurable timelines, or objectives in place before you begin.

6. Share your plan with a mentor, coach, or someone who has more experience in the planned area than you do.

7. During the meeting, evaluate the resources available to complete your plan, such as people, information, money, time, and miscellaneous resources.

8. Resist the tendency to let anything prevent the planning session from ending without the success you set as your objective.

9. Commit every plan, no matter how simple or brief, to writing.

10. Include a follow-up action/inspection/accountability process with each plan—to make sure you integrate and apply what you did during your planning session—even for your list of what you will do today.

In short: Plan. Plan. Plan. And plan some more.

---

*Without some goal and some efforts
to reach it, no man can live.*

—FYODOR DOSTOYEVSKY

CHALLENGE #17: *Gauging Information and Analysis*

Sooner or later, a manager is going to make a bad decision, take an inappropriate action, or end a project or initiative without success. This happens in the real world, folks. One of the common causes of these and other problems is that people have the perceived need to have every little piece of precise information in place before they make a decision or initiate a project.

In today's world, where everything is in a constant state of transformation and modification, it is virtually impossible for a person to predict exactly how a decision will turn out in advance. It is impractical to attempt to foresee every conceivable circumstance or condition in the early stages of any decision-making or action.

The challenge we face is how to blend the best research or information available with our experience and the will, desire, and commitment to seeing a successful outcome. There are no guarantees that an action or decision will turn out as you thought they would when you began.

Decisions, projects, programs, and plans tend to take on lives of their own as they progress. Therefore, it is necessary to be flexible, open-minded, and observant as these elements unfold.

Waiting until you have all of the information before you decide or begin may cause you to miss a window of opportunity. It could pass you by if you over-analyze the process.

Stop trying to always make right decisions. I'll bet that some of the decisions you have made that you thought were right turned out to be wrong. And I'll also bet that some of the decisions you made that you thought were wrong turned out right. So, make decisions, and then make them turn out right by your actions and commitment.

Spending too much time gathering information to try to ensure that actions turn out as planned can become a tremendous time-waster. I am not implying that you shouldn't do research, spend time in planning, and gather your forces before you begin. I am only suggesting that the time comes when you need to begin.

CHALLENGE #18: *Setting Accurate Goals and Forecasts*

Top-down goal-setting and forecasting, which can be defined as a situation in which management sets goals for lower-level employees to achieve, is a surefire way to ensure that there is a lack of ownership, commitment, and reliable participation in any corporate goals, projects, initiatives, and decisions. When goals or objectives are set top-down, there is no guarantee that they will be met, because many employees will feel that without having contributed to setting them, they are not responsible for achieving or supporting them. And when goals or objectives are established bottom-up—that is, individuals at lower levels in the organization commit to what they can do to achieve goals, there is no guarantee that they will meet the needs, criteria, or expectations of senior management.

The only effective way to ensure that management's expectations and objectives are met and that employees take ownership of them is to institute a process that combines top-down and bottom-up approaches.

A blending of top-down vision, direction, and leadership with bottom-up reality will tend to create more empowered employees. These employees will take ownership and responsibility of the top-down decisions and actions when they know that their input is taken into consideration.

There are many reasons why organizations feel that top-down forecasting and goal-setting are the best ways to achieve corporate success. It is unfortunate, however, that managers who approach the process in this way usually end up frustrated with results that are less than expected, disappointed with the outcomes, and often have to apologize for or defend the lack of success.

When your philosophy is purely top-down, you can be sure that employees will feel invalidated, irrelevant, and unimportant. When employees feel less than worthwhile, they will tend to perform their roles and tasks in a less than worthwhile or acceptable manner. However, when you include the people who must support, influence, or carry out the objectives or programs, it tends to motivate them, improve employee performance, and contribute to their sense of value to the organization.

CHALLENGE #19: *Assuming Unforeseen Outcomes*

All assumptions are dangerous, even this one. So when managers assume their plans will be successful, the outcome can be lethal.

If you haven't figured it out yet, an underlying premise of this book is that managing uncertainty, along with flexibility and dexterity, is a critical trait for managers to possess in order to be successful.

Effective planning is a huge challenge because inherent in planning are several factors such as:
- Lack of control of future outcomes
- Lack of certainty regarding conditions along the way
- Lack of consistent human reactions or responses to similar circumstances

When you assume a plan is going to be successful, you are presuming that every aspect of your plan, as well as uncontrollable events, will be under your total dominance at all times. If you must assume, I would much prefer you to believe that your plans will explode at the seams at any minute and prepare yourself accordingly. I am not implying any negativity here. But you need to understand that whenever you try to pull together a variety of internal and external factors, circumstances, people, or groups, sooner or later, one or more of them is going to disappoint you and directly or indirectly contribute to a different outcome than the one you planned for.

Planning is not an exact science, nor is it an art form. It is a unique balance of insight, intuition, experience, guesswork, creative thinking, understanding, positive anticipation, and problem-solving techniques. All planning, to be successful, must consider the many uncontrollable realities, remote possibilities, and uncertainties. Assume that there is no built-in guarantee that a plan will be successful, and stay in touch to deal with its development.

CHALLENGE #20: *Estimating the Resources and Time Needed for a Successful Plan*

Two elements can contribute to the successful outcome of any plan—accurately estimating the time you will need to achieve the desired results and correctly analyzing what resources you will need. Resources can include the people necessary to ensure that the plan, project, or initiative will have favorable consequences; the materials and equipment required; and the commitment to the plan's processes, strategies, and objectives by everyone involved. When you underestimate the resources you will need when you first begin implementing a plan, you can be sure that there will be increased stress, communication breakdowns, lack of motivation, or other negative circumstances as the plan unfolds.

Regardless of whether the planning is for a merger, acquisition, new product release, policy change or implementation, or various short- or long-term plans, some possible outcomes will be the same. These could be: less than desired results, abandonment of the plan, failure, or the need for additional resources of people, money, and time.

Plans gone astray—whether they started well or not—send a message to employees that management is not in touch with the realities necessary to ensure a successful outcome. This can contribute to the employees' lack of continued confidence and trust in management and its decisions, actions, or leadership.

Meet this challenge by putting in the time and effort, not only to state objectives that are clear, worthwhile, and sensible, but also to adequately assess the resources needed for an effective and successful outcome. This will build your employees' appreciation for the intelligence and foresight of the management team and company leadership.

CHALLENGE #21: *Reducing Crisis Management through Strategic Planning and Strategic Doing*

It is critical that managers and their organizations remain flexible, poised to react, ready to shed old baggage quickly, and change course on a dime. Therefore, constant high-adrenaline crisis management can often seem like an attractive way to run a business. In simple terms, crisis-management mode means that you wait until something happens, and then you react to it.

This type of management philosophy or business culture is associated with high costs. These can include:

1. A need to always be in the right place at the right time in order to know what is going on.
2. Consistently solving the same problems over and over again.
3. A "here-we-go-again" culture.
4. Lots of "we and they" disconnect (When a group or department is at odds for any reason, they may tend to be more concerned about the success of their own department, rather than the success of the entire organization.).
5. Poor communication throughout the organization
6. Highly stressed employees.
7. Low morale and excessive employee turnover.
8. Unjustified, increasing costs of doing business.
9. Inconsistent customer satisfaction.
10. Lost customers.
11. Antagonistic suppliers or vendors.

12. Frustrated or dissatisfied dealers, distributors, or franchisees.

In contrast, strategic planning addresses change-on-demand situations, but without the wear and tear of being in constant crisis. From my many years of facilitating corporate strategic planning events and following up on the commitments and actions that were driven by these plans, I can tell you that strategic planning also requires strategic doing—that is, everyone doing the right things (what) in the right way (how). Strategic doing is successfully and profitably connecting products or services to customers' wants and needs, both now and in the future.

I have developed six key principles to consider when developing a strategic approach to business development and growth. They are:

1. Keep your strategy simple, clear, and easy to implement, understand, and inspect.
2. If "it isn't happening," look *up* the ladder rather than down.
3. The project also requires believing and doing it with passion, commitment, and resolve.
4. The purpose is to successfully connect products and services to customers and markets, in the short term as well as the long term.
5. People and departments must be held accountable to ensure that the strategy is being implemented.
6. Everyone needs to buy into your result. This requires senior management unity and a single voice.

So, why not ask yourself the following questions (just for a starter, folks):

1. What is the problem?
2. Define what "it" is.
3. Who is it a problem for? (Customers, suppliers, employees, management, or shareholders, for example.)
4. Why is it a problem?
5. Is it a new problem or a recurring one?
6. If it is a recurring one, why hasn't it been fixed yet?
7. What would the business or the department in question look like if it weren't a problem?
8. What needs to be done to fix it? When? Why? By whom?
9. Who needs to take ownership of it?
10. What will the outcomes be if it isn't taken care of?

Ready to read on?

Plans get you into things, but you have to work your way out.

—WILL ROGERS

CHALLENGE #22: *Promoting Strategic Direction*

Intelligent, talented, and successful executives accurately see their organizations for what they really are. This is most often noticeable in the area of strategic direction—or the lack of it.

Let's take a brief look at the fourteen principles that promote validity in strategic direction and focus—or what I choose to call the Primary Strategic Driving Force of the organization:

1. Your best shot at succeeding is with a clearly developed and communicated strategic direction and focus.

2. Your senior management team must buy into it.

3. Your middle management team or employees must be involved in your strategy development process.

4. Your employees must understand it, believe it, embrace it, and use it as their benchmark in decisions, actions, and behaviors. (This takes more than having your strategy posted on a wall or banner in your office.)

5. The strategies of all business units must be clear and compatible with the corporate strategy.

6. Your strategy is developed or determined throughout the year, not just at a once-a-year retreat or planning event.

7. Your strategy is revisited on a frequent basis.

8. Your strategy never depends on, or is driven by, your competitors, current market indicators, your past performance, the government, investors, or current operational initiatives.

9. The notion that your top management team actually sets your strategy can be true, but don't get lulled into the attitude that this is definitely true. It may be an illusion. (It could be a board of directors or the marketplace, a group of your top customers, or a financial organization that actually owns the company.)

10. Your strategy drives your long-range planning. At the risk of sounding redundant: planning should focus on the how, and strategy should focus on the what. If you will keep asking yourself, "Are we talking about how or what?" you can stay focused on the strategy and not let the plans drive the strategy.

11. Strategy is not the same as a long-term plan. Just because you have a five-year plan doesn't mean you have a five-year strategy. Most long-term plans tend to be operationally focused. Long-range operational thinking (the how) may be substituting for long-range strategic thinking (the what).

12. The best time to think about and discuss strategy is when you are on top, in good financial shape, not when you are running for your life to stay ahead of the pack.

13. Your top management team is dedicated, talented, bright, and experienced enough to set, communicate, and implement your corporate strategy with integrity and congruence.

14. Strategic planning is essential even for a small business (less than fifty employees).

Understand and implement these principles and you will be a master of the challenges of planning.

---

*Four steps to achievement:
plan purposefully, prepare prayerfully,
proceed positively, pursue persistently.*
—WILLIAM WARD

CHAPTER 4

HIRING CHALLENGES

Business is about people. But if you were to look closely at Corporate America, you might be deceived. It could appear at first glance that business today is about:

- Money and profits
- Advances in technology
- Innovation and change
- Exporting jobs to other countries
- Equipment that replaces people
- Greed at the top of the corporate ladder
- Power, ego, and manipulation
- Disregard for employees and their needs, dreams, and hopes

Now, please keep in mind that I am not talking about all of Corporate America, just some of it. And I am not implying that it is all bad. What I want you to recognize is that the organizations that treat their employees with respect, trust, compassion, and understanding tend to make more money, have more influence, accomplish more, grow, and experience a general condition of enduring success.

I don't care how much technology advances or how much money you make, business is and always will be about people. Therefore, the challenge today is to consistently find, develop, retain, and cultivate the best employees. It is no wonder that I hear over and over again, "Good help is hard to find," given today's circumstances. Some issues that affect how companies recruit, hire, train, and retain employees include:

- The graying generation who are leaving the workforce—either through retirement or dying
- The Baby Boomers who are leaving Corporate America
- Immigration laws and challenges
- The attitudes of the X- and Y-Generations
- The continuously rising cost of living
- The increase in entry-level jobs that many people will not take
- The exporting of technology, customer service, accounting, and manufacturing jobs to foreign countries to realize cost savings

There are several interviewing and hiring techniques, attitudes, and concepts that, when not followed, can lead to poor hiring decisions as well as a potential discrimination lawsuit if you are not careful. This chapter will address some of the more vital ones. If you believe that hiring is one of your weaker skills, I would urge you to register for one of my Management/Leadership Boot Camps, hire me as a business coach, or bring me in-house to conduct a custom, all-day session on this critical topic area.

Finding and hiring good employees does not have to be an ongoing problem. All that is necessary is to understand some fundamental rules and approaches and then practice them routinely.

The biggest human temptation is to settle for too little.

—Thomas Merton

CHALLENGE #23: *Finding Good Employees*

Potential good employees are everywhere. A recent study I read said that more than 70 percent of employees were unhappy in their jobs and would change organizations for the right opportunities. Keep in mind that people don't quit jobs; they quit managers.

There are a variety of sources of qualified candidates for any position you have available. Listed in order of effectiveness are a few to consider:

1. Using current employees as recruiters for new employees. Some organizations compensate employees for this activity while others know that if you have satisfied, happy, and productive employees, these people want to surround themselves with people they know, like, and trust, and will invite certain people to join them at their current place of employment.

2. Scouring the marketplace for currently employed employees at your suppliers, customers, competitors, or other local businesses where you have contacts. I am not recommending that you actively proselytize, turning your customers or suppliers into enemies because you are stealing their best employees. The key here is to create a corporate culture and reputation where you are known as the ideal place to work. In other words, turn your organization into a magnet that attracts the type of employees you want so you don't have to go prowling the marketplace for them.

3. Using temp-to-permanent agencies. These employees will work for you on a contract basis. If you don't like a temporary employee for whatever reason, send them home and tell the agency you want a different one. There will be no hassle, no obligations, and no chance of finding out you made a bad hire and that it's too late to fix it. However, if you like the employee and you feel they are a fit for your organization, you can negotiate with the agency to hire them as a full-time employee if the employee is also interested.

The worst place to find candidates is in the local newspaper. And even the Internet websites that offer these services are rapidly falling into the same category.

CHALLENGE #24: *Refusing to Hire under Pressure*

Hiring under pressure is a common mistake many managers make when they are in a hurry to get an employee in place or a decision made. When you hire under pressure because you have an opening that needs to be filled now, you will tend to hire beneath your standards and make a hiring mistake. Ever done it? Most managers have at some point, whether it was due to an open sales territory, a support staff person who suddenly quit, or the result of a new client that required additional staff to service him or her.

Without a hiring template or process, managers often tend to make hiring decisions—and mistakes—based on the "halo effect" (the potential hire just "feels" so good) or on their emotional state at the time of the interview. This can lead to a poor hire—not that the person is necessarily a bad potential employee, but they may not be right for your organization.

When you hire under pressure, you may overlook the lack of necessary experience, skills, or attitudes and try to force a fit. Rather than getting someone into a job quickly, it is a far better policy to not rush or deviate from the process that you normally follow. This is why it is important to have a hiring template or process.

Your hiring template should include such things as:
- Steps you will take and when you will take them
- Time frames
- Ideal candidate traits and attitudes
- Questions you will ask

- Compensation issues and how they will be handled
- Other factors that you feel are important

Your hiring process should also specify hiring everyone on a ninety-day probationary period. If during this early period of employment you discover that a hiring mistake was made, you can fix it quickly without adding stress to your HR department or setting yourself up for a wrongful termination claim or suit.

Always use an outside independent testing or employee evaluation service to give you an impartial look at the candidate.

CHALLENGE #25: *Hiring Attitudes and Not Skills*

It is easier to teach skills to a new employee than to change his or her attitudes. Many managers feel that finding the right skill combination in a new employee is the best philosophy to have when recruiting. But many of these same managers have learned the hard way that just because someone has the skills doesn't mean he or she will use them.

Several years ago when I was hiring an administrative assistant, I interviewed several qualified candidates. Each of them possessed the required typing ability, computer knowledge, and administrative skills. The one I selected actually had the slowest typing speed, but the best attitude. Why did I do that?

I have discovered that an employee who can type 120 words per minute but who has a bit of an attitude problem will hardly ever achieve that speed while working. By the same token, someone with a great attitude who can type only fifty words per minute will always be trying to improve his or her speed.

Call it what you want—arrogance, ego, pride, insecurity, low self-esteem, no self-confidence—but sooner or later, these people with emotional or mental issues will become untrainable from a skill standpoint.

People develop attitudes over a lifetime, and you are not going to change them in the short time an employee might be with you. By the same token, if you hire a person with a great attitude, I guarantee this employee will push you and make you look good. Before you know it, the employee will outgrow the position and want, as well as need, to move on. Everyone wins in the process.

Avoiding a hiring mistake can save you lots of grief, wasted training time, and negative impact on other employees and customers, not to mention the possibility of a legal or financial fiasco when you need to terminate them. Don't risk it. The price is too high.

CHALLENGE #26: *Conducting an Effective Interview Process*

One of the best things you can do to ensure that you do not take a haphazard approach to interviewing is to follow a few basic steps. Here are twenty to consider:

1. Be professional in every way.
2. Always have a written and current description of the position.
3. Work from a set of standard questions that you ask each candidate. This list should contain anywhere from fifteen to twenty-five questions. These same questions should be repeated during each interview you conduct with each applicant, maybe in a different order, but the same questions, nonetheless.
4. Decide that you are going to interview the person, not hire him or her. Remember that the resume is a balance sheet without the negatives, which will help you decide whether or not the candidate is right for your company.
5. Look for traits, experience, and skills that match the requirements of the position, not just general qualities.
6. Take notes, but never on the resume.
7. Observe what issues the candidate seems most interested in. Poor candidates focus on compensation and benefits. Good candidates focus on the job and opportunity.
8. Hire happy people if you want happy employees.
9. Pay attention to subtle signals. People always try to put their best foot forward during an interview, but observe, for example, if there are coffee stains on the resume or

the person is late. (Do people do these dumb things? Oh, yes.)

10. Don't break the law with illegal questions.

11. Get written permission to check several professional references (not their best friend, parents, or neighbors).

12. Interview a candidate two to three times. Also, it is prudent to have one other person interview them as well.

13. Pay attention to how long the interviews run. It is better to have three one-hour interviews than one three-hour interview.

14. Write an interview summary immediately after the interview for future comparison and reference.

15. Quote salary on weekly terms.

16. Don't send mixed messages or allude to future facts about salary. For example, saying that all of your salespeople, after one year, are making over $100,000 a year. You are sending the subtle message that the applicant will be, too, and if things don't turn out as expected, you'll end up with a demotivated or even an ex-employee.

17. Hire the person who wants the job the most and who intuitively feels right. Keep in mind that when all things are relatively equal—such as experience, skills, attitudes, references, talent, the resume, and so on—how well the person will fit into the organization is important.

18. Ask the person who is going to supervise the employee to make the hiring decision.

19. Look for your own replacement.

20. Interview at least one candidate (whether you have an opening or not) at least once a month. This practice will help you keep your interviewing skills sharp and effective.

Imagination in business is the ability to perceive opportunity.

—ABRAHAM ZALEZNIK

CHALLENGE #27: *Establishing Clear Employee Expectations*

Getting your new employee off to a positive start is a function of many factors. These can include:

- How they perceived the hiring process
- The expectations that were shared from both the candidate and the interviewer
- The match of skills and attitudes of the candidate with the position
- How the new employee is indoctrinated into your organization and its culture
- The content and delivery of initial training

One of the most critical factors has to do with expectations of both employee and employer. The candidate will have expectations about the organization and the manager, and the manager and organization will likewise have expectations of the new employee. Having unrealized expectations about another person is one of the biggest causes of stress and frustration in relationships or employment.

Let's say for a moment that, based upon conversations held during the interview process, a new employee expects that he will be given several weeks of training and indoctrination about the organization and about his role there. Upon entering the real world of his new position, for whatever reason, he receives only a few days of training and is then thrust into the throes of the position and the responsibilities it entails.

Right out of the gate, this employee is justified in being frustrated because commitments were made that were not honored. As a result, he may find himself in the difficult position of being expected to perform without the training needed to be productive. This simple scenario occurs frequently in hundreds of organizations every day, and it is only one example of possible perceived expectations. The manager expects performance and doesn't get it. The employee expects the tools necessary to be productive and doesn't get them. I am sure you can see how the outcome in this situation will be less than desirable.

The key to avoiding such situations is to ensure that both the manager and candidate are clear about each other's expectations before the employee begins. This process should take place either on the employee's first day (before he gets into the groove) or as the last step in the interview process, once an offer has been made, accepted, and a start date determined.

This simple yet effective step can contribute to the success and productivity of your new employee as well as reduce your stress and frustration. I further recommend that you get these mutual expectations in writing so that there is no room for misunderstanding later.

What concerns me is not the way things are,
but rather the way people think things are.

—EPICTETUS

CHAPTER 5

DELEGATING CHALLENGES

One of the greatest challenges a manager faces is how to delegate tasks, responsibilities, or outcomes. In order to be an effective manager, you need to be able and willing to delegate, as well as know what you can delegate, when you can delegate it, and whom you can delegate it to. The role of a manager is not to do it, but to get other people to do it.

There are exceptions to what a manager can delegate, however. Personal producing managers (sales, customer service, and human resources) and self-employed business owners who have small staffs cannot delegate everything. But even these people can delegate some things to someone else. You can use subcontractors, cottage help (people who are not employees, agents, or contract help), or temporary employees.

Here are a few of the keys to effective delegation:

1. Delegate it if someone else can do it, wants to do it, needs to do it, or likes to do it.

2. When you delegate responsibility, also delegate the authority to use the resources to get it done.

3. Delegate results, not the methods.
4. Use delegation as an employee development tool.
5. When you delegate something, don't take it back.
6. Ensure the person understands what and why you have delegated to them.
7. Communicate clear instructions, expectations, and guidelines.
8. Put it in writing, if necessary.
9. Ask for regular written or verbal reports.
10. Set benchmarks or checkpoints with designees, and then leave them alone.
11. Recognize and accept that it won't be done the way you would do it.
12. Resist the tendency to over-inspect.
13. Remember what you delegated and to whom.
14. Reinforce positive results, and give corrective feedback on negative results.
15. See any employee failure as a necessary, positive step if people are to be expected to stretch, learn, and grow in their expertise.

As a manager, one of your biggest frustrations is probably the lack of time to perform all of the work required of you. Therefore, think of delegation as simply giving yourself the opportunity to spend more time in the vital areas of your job, such as planning, organizing, inspecting, coaching, innovating, and developing people.

Why not take a serious look at how you are spending your time and what tasks you are involved in that could be delegated to someone else? Track your use of time for a week, logging all of the repetitive activities, problem-solving routines, crisis-management issues, and routine stuff. Then, at the end of the week, ask yourself these questions. Could someone else (or some other department) have done this? What did I not complete because of these actions? I personally guarantee that you can free up at least an hour a day if you will find creative ways to delegate.

If you want to increase your success rate, double your failure rate.

—Tom Watson

CHALLENGE #28: *Trusting Your Employees*

One of the vital qualities that contribute to employees' effectiveness is knowing that their managers and organizations trust them. Employees who believe they are not trusted will exhibit certain negative traits and behaviors (for example, increased negative gossip, poor productivity, tardiness, increased conflict, etc.) that can have a derogatory impact on organization performance, market share, customer loyalty, market perceptions, growth, and profitability.

I believe that most employees go to work every day wanting to do a good job. Sure, there are some employees who are constant discipline problems or are less than productive, but you have resources for dealing with those behaviors.

So, why don't managers or organizations trust their good employees? Here are a few reasons:
- Managers with hidden or personal agendas
- Insecure managers
- Managers who are control freaks
- Managers with out-of-control egos
- Secretive corporate cultures
- Organizations with a heavy top-down management style

Remember, managers manage, executives lead and set vision, but the work in all organizations is done at the employee level. If these employees don't feel they are trusted to use resources and make decisions or that they are empowered to perform, I will guarantee that you will end up with an organization or department that is stuck in counterproductive policies, procedures, and behaviors.

Trust men and they will be true to you;
treat them greatly and they will show
themselves great.

—RALPH WALDO EMERSON

CHALLENGE #29: *Delegating Results rather than Processes and Methods*

There are a number of advantages to delegating tasks to employees, the least of which is to give them opportunities for career development. When you delegate an assignment to one of your staff, you are sending a loud and clear message: "I want you to take on additional responsibility that will help you learn new skills and expand your horizons."

There is a right and wrong way to delegate anything to anyone though. The wrong way is to delegate the how, why, and where. The right way is to delegate the what. Let me explain.

When you give an assignment or task to an employee and then proceed to tell them how to do it, you may as well have done it yourself. Giving them the how says you don't trust them to do it right—or even better than you've done it.

When you delegate anything, the purpose is to have someone else do it. Giving the person or group too many guidelines, rules, and how-to's prevents them from using their own creativity, problem-solving skills, imagination, experience, and decision-making ability. Yes, they should be given some parameters, such as completion date, boundaries, benchmarks, timelines, check-in points, resource restrictions, decision limitations, and expected results. But if you give too much of the how, I guarantee that your objective to help your employee further develop will be limited at best.

Delegating is a tremendous motivational tool, but it can also be a demotivational tool. Telling employees you trust them but then behaving in a way that demonstrates you really don't will backfire every time. Delegating results and not methods is an effective way to send positive messages to your employee.

Remember, there are other ways to do things than your way. You have to be willing to give up control, your ego, and maybe even your righteousness about how things should be done. Who knows? Your employees may even do it better than you would have, had you not delegated the assignment at all. The question is: can you handle that? If not, better keep on reading. A general rule to keep in mind is to delegate little things at first and then increase the degree of responsibility as the employee improves and demonstrates the necessary confidence, skills, and motivation.

Some of us will do our jobs well and some will not, but we will be judged by only one thing—the result.

—Vince Lombardi

CHALLENGE #30: *Setting Clear Parameters and Expectations*

If you are traditionally not one who delegates, but you have decided that it is a skill you need to develop, there are a few things you might want to keep in mind. Or if you delegate routinely, you might find a few techniques here that might improve your results.

Before delegating a task, it is important to lay out the guidelines and expectations you have for results. Here are some of my guidelines for setting expectations and outcomes:

1. Meet with employees, and ask them if they feel confident that they can handle the assignment.
2. Ask them what roadblocks they think they might encounter and how they would handle them.
3. Help them determine what resources might be needed to carry out the task.
4. Set up midpoint check-in times in advance so they don't think you are constantly looking over their shoulders during performance.
5. Establish clear definitions of the results you desire.
6. Determine the boundaries of responsibility.
7. Tell them that you won't be interfering with their methods as long as they stay within the determined boundaries.
8. Advise them that they are free to come to you at any time with questions, suggestions, or feedback.
9. Support their methods, decisions, and processes.
10. Celebrate their successes.

11. Ask them to give you a review of what they would do differently if they could begin all over again.
12. Give them an even bigger task the next time.

Remember, the more you can delegate, the more time you have for your own critical responsibilities as a manager.

CHALLENGE #31: *Giving Authority with Responsibility*

If you want demotivated employees, delegate the responsibility for a task, project, or assignment to them, and don't give them the authority to make decisions, use resources, solve problems, or find creative ways to get it done. This is the fast track to ensure that you lower morale and diminish your employee's motivation and commitment to your corporate mission and purpose.

If you as a manager have ever had a project or process delegated to you by your supervisor and been given the responsibility for outcomes, but not the authority to get it done, you know exactly how your employees feel if you have ever done that to them. Why would a manager give an employee a task or responsibility and then not give them the authority to carry it out? Some reasons include:

- Perceived loss of control
- Concern that it might not be done correctly
- Uneasiness that designees might make a wrong decision
- Fear that they might overextend resources
- Discomfort that they might take too long getting it done
- Worry that they might do a better job than the manager

Let me give you an example of a typical scenario in which authority is delegated with responsibility:

Bill is a customer service representative for his company. His manager asked him to solve a problem for one of the company's biggest customers. Bill's manager told him to do whatever was necessary to satisfy this customer in this situation. Bill waives the shipping costs and restocking fees that would normally apply, which were a significant amount. The customer is satisfied and happy to continue doing business with Bill's company. Bill's manager is proud of this resolution and tells Bill so. Gain in motivation? Gain in productivity? Gain in dedication? Yes. Yes. Yes.

CHALLENGE #32: *Refusing to Take It Back after You Have Delegated It*

Managers take things back in subtle and often discreet ways, and also in overt and blatant ways. In either case, the outcome is the same: they are telling their employees that they don't trust them, have confidence in them, or believe in them. Any of these three is a recipe for short-term—and even long-term—disaster.

Taking back delegated tasks can happen anytime from right after the employee has been given the task to just about the time the individual has almost completed it. But there never is a good time to take back something you have delegated. Whenever you do it, you will still damage the employee's self-esteem and self-confidence.

Catch yourself if you:

- Tell the employee that the expectations have changed and the project must be completed sooner than was planned, so you will finish it up.
- Tell the employee that you need him to work on a different project or task that is even more important than the one he is working on (which may or may not be true) and that you will finish up where he left off.

Because of all the values that can be realized by delegating tasks to employees, which were mentioned earlier in this chapter, smart managers will not take back delegated tasks even when:

- The employee isn't doing it as fast as they think he should.

- The employee isn't doing it the way they want it done.
- They don't like the way it is being done.
- It isn't being done according to their definition of right.
- They have decided they don't like giving up control after all.

I hope it is irresistibly clear by now that managers who empower employees, departments, and any group of employees by delegating more tasks improve performance and increase organizational effectiveness. It can also improve teambuilding and corporate communication.

CHAPTER 6

FEEDBACK CHALLENGES

Employees want to know how they are doing—whether it is good work or work that needs improvement. No one likes to operate in a vacuum. Smart managers are willing and able to give timely, accurate, and effective feedback to their employees. There are two types of feedback: positive, which provides recognition and shows appreciation for work well-done, and negative, which focuses on needed corrections or behavior modification.

There is a very simple management principle that hundreds of organizations and thousands of managers, executives, or business owners just don't get: if you want positive behavior repeated, reward it. Let people know you appreciate their effort, dedication, energy, and time commitment. If you are getting negative behavior and you ignore it—it too will be repeated.

This is one of the concerns I have about annual reviews. If you have employee behavior that needs modification, don't wait a year to fix it.

Part of the problem with negative feedback is that managers see it only as punishment or discipline. Negative feedback is designed to change or correct behavior that is inappropriate or wrong, not to punish.

Always give negative feedback in private. Give positive feedback both publicly and privately. Public recognition of positive behavior builds the self-esteem of the individual receiving it and sends a message to other employees that this behavior is what you desire and are willing to reward. Giving positive feedback in private once in a while also sends a positive message to other employees that Sally or Bob is not being disciplined every time you call them into your office.

Surveys have shown that most employees value praise, recognition, and appreciation above higher wages and benefits. When managers have been surveyed, they believed that most employees see higher wages, job security, and benefits as more important than this positive feedback.

Start giving more positive feedback, and you will be amazed at the positive results you will get. Start giving more negative feedback when appropriate, and watch productivity improve.

The willingness to give positive and negative feedback is often the outcome of your corporate culture. Remember, all corporate culture, communication, and attitudes are top-down. You can't fix these issues bottom-up.

Champions know that success is inevitable; that there is no such thing as failure, only feedback. They know that the best way to forecast the future is to create it.

—Michael J. Gelb

CHALLENGE #33: *Handling Employee Mistakes and Failures*

Employees are bound to make mistakes and sometimes fail. What are your attitudes or responses when an employee makes a mistake or fails at some activity or project? Here are some of the choices. You can:

- Get angry
- Blame them
- Discipline them
- Isolate them
- Fire them
- Feel sorry for them
- Help them learn from it
- Praise them for their efforts
- Encourage them

What can you add to the list? Did you see your typical attitude or response here? If not, what is yours?

There are basically two ways any manager, supervisor, or executive can act when an employee makes a mistake or fails. He or she can:

- React positively with coaching, training, and encouragement
- React negatively with discipline, blame, and anger

Which do you think is the smart response? Why?

A manager's personality (who the person is) rather than tenure seems to be the key factor here. We can't separate who we are—our attitudes, values, beliefs, expectations, opinions, history, and feelings—from our roles or positions in life. If you are a nice person, you will tend to be a nice manager. If you are an unpleasant person, it is no surprise that you will tend to be an unpleasant manager. So, who are you? What kind of manager are you?

CHALLENGE #34: *Giving Both Positive and Negative Feedback*

Do you use Seagull Management as your dominant style? What is Seagull Management? Let me give you a scenario: The typical manager flies into the department, rapidly flapping his wings, while squawking loudly enough to be heard in the next building. He then squats, shakes his butt, craps all over his employees, and flies out of the department. For those of you with less vivid imaginations, a seagull manager is one who always delivers only bad news and never offers praise, positive feedback, or recognition.

Ever worked for someone with this approach to management? Demotivating, wasn't it? Many managers just don't get it. Most employees would like to be effective, do a good job, and get their work done on time and correctly. The problem is, many organizations sabotage employee performance top-down and refuse to look in the mirror to determine the cause of this situation.

Over the years, I have consulted with hundreds of organizations in a variety of industries worldwide. I found that one of the most common critical mistakes managers make every day is to give too little positive feedback and recognition and poorly deliver negative feedback or discipline.

You get the behavior you reward. Behavior reinforced is behavior repeated. What goes around comes around. It doesn't matter how you say it, the result is always the same. If you don't like the behavior you are getting, don't look just at your employees. Look also at your management style, corporate culture, and communication patterns to determine where part of the problem lies. Remember: You will get more of the behavior you want with positive feedback than by giving only negative feedback.

Human behavior flows from three main sources: desire, emotion, and knowledge.

—PLATO

CHALLENGE #35: *Giving Enough Positive Recognition and Appreciation*

Studies over the years have indicated that the one thing most employees want more of and tend to get less than enough of is recognition and appreciation for the work they do. Sure, every employee gets a regular paycheck from his or her employer that is the payment for his or her services, skills, time, and energy. But let me ask you this: Do you have a boss or supervisor? Even if you are the CEO or chairman, there is someone higher than you on the food chain. This could be your board or your customer—who pays your salary, overhead, and profits. (Lose enough customers and you are out of business.) Even at the top, wouldn't you like some positive recognition or appreciation once in a while for a job well done?

Everyone wants to be validated. Everyone wants to feel worthwhile. And everyone wants to feel like they are making a contribution that makes a difference.

I will guarantee you that at least one of your employees has done something in the past week that they feel is worthy of some special thanks, appreciation, or even recognition, but didn't get. What do you think will happen to their loyalty, motivation, passion, and commitment over time if this is a frequent occurrence for them?

There is a simple concept to keep in mind here. As I stated in Challenge #34, behavior reinforced is behavior repeated. If you have an employee or group of employees who are behaving in a way that contributes to effectiveness, growth, or success, wouldn't you want that behavior to continue?

Even increase it? The one surefire way to accomplish this is to give recognition and appreciation when the demonstrated behavior is the behavior you want.

In his bestselling classic, *The One-Minute Manager*, Ken Blanchard says it so simply: "Catch people doing things right. Then acknowledge it and recognize it, and you will be amazed at how it will continue."

CHALLENGE #36: *Inspecting What You Expect*

Among the most important roles of any manager is the willingness and ability to inspect performance according to expected standards, and the commitment to reinforce what is learned through feedback, consistent messages, and coaching.

Know this for sure: if it isn't happening in your organization or department, but there is a policy or procedure in place that requires it to happen, then something is falling through the cracks somewhere. If you don't inspect what you expect, you no longer have the right to expect it. Inspecting what you expect is simply holding people accountable for behaviors, actions, attitudes, and decisions. If you don't inspect these, you have no way of knowing whether they are happening or not.

Here is a quick example. Years ago, I had a policy with my support staff that every book order would be sent out with the following: an order form, a brochure of my services, a thank-you note, and a free item of some kind. I placed a bogus order on the telephone one day, and when I received the package, several of these items were missing. When I asked my staff about this, they said that they had forgotten to include them. I have to wonder how many orders were shipped without these items before I checked on my staff.

If you are not inspecting it, it is not happening consistently. If you are not reinforcing your training and coaching, it is not happening consistently.

There are only three ways to ensure that your employees know what to do and how to do it:

1. Teach, train, and educate them.
2. Reinforce the training with meetings, assignments, coaching, and support materials, for example, books and CDs.
3. Inspect regularly whatever you expect (believe) is happening (should be happening).

CHALLENGE #37: *Conducting Regular Reviews*

Thousands of employees perform tasks and duties daily, unaware of how they are doing according to the systems, structure, or expectations of their management staff. As a result, there are hundreds of man/woman-hours wasted each day in redundant activities, as well as a tremendous waste of time and capital resources.

All of this can be avoided by a constant vigilance regarding employee behavior and performance. The time to modify behavior is not once a year at an annual review. Incorrect behaviors or attitudes should be corrected when they happen. The annual review should be more of an overall career path discussion than an attempt to "fix" the employee.

Most managers who conduct employee reviews have never been trained on how to conduct them. As a result, they end up wasting time, and the review can even have a negative impact on the employee's attitudes and future performance.

One of the questions I always ask when conducting confidential interviews in preparation for an in-house training program is "does your organization have a formal review policy?" Seventy percent of the time, for the past ten years, the answer has been no. Of the 30 percent who answer yes, I ask, "Is it effective, timely, or of any value to you as an employee or the organization?" Eighty percent have said it is of little value. It is merely an exercise.

What about your own review policy, program, or strategy? How would you describe it? How would your employees respond to my questions? It might be an interesting exercise!

There are a number of excellent books, seminars, and audio and video tapes on how to plan and conduct employee reviews. Mastering skills in this area as a manager may increase your number of good employees, as well as boost morale.

CHALLENGE #38: *Having a Systematic Review Process*

For a number of years, I have been teaching a simple, yet successful, coaching and review process to improve employee and management effectiveness. It is called the 3/3/3. I will briefly describe how it works.[1]

The purpose of the 3/3/3 Quarterly Review

In order to improve both management and employee effectiveness, it is essential that employees be empowered to give bottom-up feedback to their manager. This feedback can be invaluable for a manager's continued development. It is also important that employees be willing to evaluate themselves for ongoing improvement and attitude and behavior modification, if this is necessary.

Generally speaking, most employees would like to have more frequent feedback (both positive and negative) on their performance than once a year. They want to know how they are doing. Remember, you get the behavior you reward—and reinforced behavior will contribute to repeated similar behavior. The purpose of the 3/3/3 review is to develop a consistent and ongoing bottom-up feedback process, as well as the self-discovery both the manager and the employee need to help improve or modify behavior and/or attitudes.

The 3/3/3 method is easy to perform and, over time, will ensure that managers are in touch with the reality and the

[1] If you would like to see a copy of the instrument I have created for this process, to determine if you would like to order some for your employees, please visit my website, www.timconnor.com. It's only $15.00 and the package is good for a year's worth of quarterly reviews for both the manager and his or her direct reports.

impact of their behavior and that their employees begin to take full responsibility for their own development.

How 3/3/3 process works

The first number 3 in the 3/3/3 series stands for "every three months." This is how often you should meet with each of your direct reports. These sessions should be done in person and can last anywhere from twenty minutes to one hour. The second 3 represents the three things the employee believes or feels you are doing that are getting in the way of his effectiveness. The third 3 stands for three things the employee feels or believes he is doing that are getting in the way of the employee's effectiveness.

During the first session, you explain to the employee how the process works and its value to you, to him, and to the organization. Here's how it goes: you first ask your employee to tell you three things that he believes or feels you are doing that are getting in the way of his effectiveness. Discussion follows. After he gives you three, you then ask him, "Is there anything else?" Discussion follows. So you could possibly end up with four or more things you need to address. (Please note that depending on your organizational culture, you may or may not want to discuss the 3/3/3 process with your employee before the actual meeting and let him prepare beforehand, if you feel that it might help the process, add to his comfort, or produce more honest answers.)

Next, you ask your employee, "What are three things that you feel or believe you are doing that are getting in the way of your effectiveness or success, the success of the department, or the success of the organization?" Discussion follows. After he gives you three—if one of the three does not include one that you feel needs his attention—you can say, "There is one other thing I would like you to consider working on and that is _____." (You previously set this up—above—by asking the employee if there was anything else you were doing, after he gave you your three areas needing attention.)

Take note: At no time in this process is there top-down feedback. This process is intended to help employees learn to change their own behavior and attitudes without you having to continue to give them top-down feedback.

After each of you has your list of three or four things that you need to work on, you can close the session with the statement, "I am going to work on my four things for the next three months; are you willing to work on yours?" This usually gets a positive response. Then you say, "Great, let's get together in three months and see what progress each of us has made."

The next thing is to empower your employees to give you feedback on how you are doing between sessions. You also can set up coaching sessions between each 3/3/3 by asking them, for example, "How do you think you are doing on number two?"

The second and subsequent sessions start out just a little differently. You begin with, "How do you feel I am doing on my three things?" Discussion follows.

Next, ask your employee, "How do you feel you are doing on your three things?" Discussion follows. Then ask, "Have

I started any new behavior(s) or developed any new attitudes during the past three months that are getting in the way of your effectiveness?" Discussion (if necessary) follows.

Next, you ask: "Do you believe you have started any new behaviors or developed any new attitudes during the past three months that you feel are preventing you from being effective or successful?" Discussion (if necessary) follows.

Remember: it is critical that you follow this format. Be sure you begin each session by asking your employees to evaluate you first, and then follow with their own self-evaluation.

The important thing is not to stop questioning. Curiosity has its own reason for existing.

—ALBERT EINSTEIN

CHALLENGE #39: *Implementing Training with Effective Coaching*

Most training does not change behavior for the long term. That is because over the course of their lives, people have formed beliefs, attitudes, and behaviors that you cannot change just because you stick them in an all-day training session to improve their sales, customer service, or management skills.

Everyone has personal agendas. Some are beneficial to the organization, while others may be destructive. The purpose of training is to give people the standards or expectations for behaviors—in other words, what to do, how to do it, when to do it, and often why to do it. But on its own, training may not stick.

To be truly effective, training must be measured, followed up, and inspected. And employees must be held accountable in order for your training investment to be worthwhile.

I have been in the training business for more than thirty years, and I can tell you that in order for your training to yield the results you want, need, or expect, your reinforcement strategy needs to include the following:
- Setting clear expectations
- Insisting on consistent follow-up coaching
- Establishing measurements
- Holding people accountable
- Using reinforcement tools such as exercises, discussions, assignments, manuals, assessment tools, books, or CDs

Follow-up coaching requires that the manager be in a position to observe behaviors, actions, activities, decisions, and results. This applies whether employees are working in close proximity or whether they are working remotely, a thousand miles away.

CHAPTER 7

MOTIVATION CHALLENGES

Motivation. Some people have more of it than others. Some people need other people or outside circumstances to get them moving, while others have an inner drive to move forward.

The word *motivation* has within it the words motiv(e) and *a(c)tion*. A motive is a purpose, a reason, a goal. And everyone knows what action is: it is doing.

Why do some people have goals and appear to move with steadfast consistency toward success while other people seem to struggle year in and year out, trying to find their destiny, purpose, or mission in life? There are no simple answers to this age-old question. That is because we are dealing with people, with human behavior that is generally not predictable or understood by most of us. I hear again and again from managers, business owners, and parents: Why did they do that? Why won't they do this?

The simple answer is that we are not dealing with computers that can be programmed. We are interacting every day with people who have emotional ups and downs, philosophical rationalizations, very personal perceptual interpretations, and often secret motives and agendas.

In the final analysis, each of us does what we do, thinks what we think, feels what we feel, believes what we believe, and acts the way we act because it serves us in some way. We may be consciously aware of these reasons, or they may be deeply imbedded in our unconscious. Either way, it makes reading people's intentions and actions a real challenge.

All appears to change when we change.

—Henri-Frédérick Amiel

CHALLENGE #40: *Motivating Employees*

I constantly hear from managers, "How do I motivate my employees?" You can't. Motivation is an inside-out individual responsibility. The challenge for a manager is to create an environment in which employees want to motivate themselves for peak performance.

There are two traditional methods of motivating employees that are being used in thousands of companies by literally millions of managers to "motivate" employees. They are: fear (or punishment) and reward (incentive). Both of these motivational environments are temporary and appeal to the outside-in need to be motivated.

Fear-based motivation relies on punishment of some kind, ranging from withdrawal of a privilege to being fired. If fear-based motivation is the dominant type of motivation you or your organization uses, I will bet you live with a great deal of frustration. People can build up immunity to your threats. And if they are not concerned about the punishment, it won't motivate them. Fear-based motivation is also negative and tends to demotivate—the opposite of what you are attempting to accomplish.

Reward- or incentive-based motivation focuses on a want or need of the employee. The problem is, if employees don't want what you are rewarding them with, guess what? It won't do any good.

Rewards or appreciation should be related to what the person wants, needs, or feels is appropriate for their behavior. A simple thank you might do it for one person, while another might want public appreciation. Others might prefer a thank-you note or even an invitation to lunch as special acknowledgment.

Still others may only respond to financial rewards. These could be anything from a couple of movie tickets to a special gift (inexpensive). Keep in mind that it's not just the financial value, but the thought and behavior you exhibit. Sometimes, just noticing and responding is often enough.

I worked with a company last year in which the average yearly sales compensation was more than $75,000 per employee. The president was frustrated because the employees' potential was in excess of $200,000 a year per employee. No additional incentives would improve performance because each of the employees was satisfied with their current compensation levels. So offering them bribes, bonuses, or nicer drapes in their office didn't get them to work harder to sell more.

There is an old saying that says, "You can lead a horse to water, but you can't make him drink." You can, however, put a little salt in his oats to make him thirsty. Why do I share this insight? Because the only motivation method that works for the long haul is turning over the responsibility of motivation to the individual. That's why it is called self-motivation. It happens from within. The key here is for managers to link their employees' personal objectives or goals to corporate goals, so that employees recognize that they can get what they want by helping the company to get what it wants.

This third type of motivation is based on a person's attitude development. Individuals do something more or better, not because you want them to or because you threaten them or promise them the moon, but because they want to.

The key role of a manager is to hire self-motivated employees. Then they need to do as little as possible to demotivate them.

Since motivation is an inside-out process, it is no wonder that many businesses have a productivity problem. They are relying on one of the two temporary methods of motivation that are outside-in.

The better solution is to create a motivational environment where people who are motivated (from the inside) do not need your threats, punishment, or rewards. They perform because they want to. That's who they are. There is another old saying I heard recently: "Don't send your ducks to eagle school. If you want eagles, hire eagles."

Motivation is a fire from within.
If someone else tries to light that fire
under you, chances are it will
burn very briefly.

—Stephen R. Covey

CHALLENGE #41: *Setting a Clear Direction and Focus*

A common problem among many businesses today is that they lack a sense of identity. In the words of one manager I interviewed last year, "I don't know who we are or where we are heading, and yet I am supposed to help us get there." These feelings are common among many workers today, whether expressed or kept silent.

A lack of communicated, understood, reinforced, and believed-in direction by employees is at the root of many organizations' real-world problems. When asked, many executives will say that the real challenges they face are: employee turnover, increased global competition, finding good employees, and government regulations. These business owners, managers, and executives believe that these critical issues they face in the marketplace today contribute to their lack of profits, slowed growth, paltry market share, or lack of competitiveness. But don't be lulled into a sense of blaming things that you cannot control. It is far better to focus on things that you can control.

The absence of clear, focused, and communicated direction and identity in an organization contributes to any one or several damaging results. I suggest you circle below those you feel may be a problem for your organization. If you are feeling really secure, give the same list to your management team and ask them to circle the items they feel need attention. If you are feeling really brave, I suggest you give the list to a representative group of employees and ask them to do the same.

Ready? Identify what pertains to you, your department, or organization:

- Poor internal communication
- Low or poor morale
- Poor employee development
- Increased employee turnover
- Difficulty in attracting new employees
- Poor productivity
- High sales costs
- Too many meetings in which nothing is accomplished
- Redundancy
- Lack of clear goals
- High receivables
- Vulnerability to competition
- Poor external communication
- Reduced sales and profits
- Reduced market share
- Lack of financial growth
- Poor customer service
- Customer dissatisfaction
- Customer turnover
- Management or senior management turnover

If this list is not enough to give you cardiac arrest, I don't know what will. Any three of the above items can put you in the dumpster. If you have more than three, please give me a call. I may be able to help you.

Destiny is not a matter of chance. It is a matter of choice. It is not something to be waited for. It is something to be achieved.

—William Jennings Bryan

CHALLENGE #42: *Empowering Employees*

Management styles contribute greatly to the corporate culture as well as to the productivity (or lack thereof) of individuals and departments. Managers who are able to empower employees, departments, and groups of employees typically can improve performance and increase organizational effectiveness. It can also create a great deal of stress and havoc if upper-level management does not totally buy into this philosophy.

What is empowerment? It is not a fad, although it seems to have gained in popularity during the past decade or two. Empowerment can be defined as being the state of feeling self-empowered so as to behave, take action, and control work and decision-making in autonomous ways. Rather than give you a narrative, though, I would prefer to share a list. I find that lists help people better identify strengths as well as weaknesses.

Empowered organizations:

1. Give authority with responsibility.
2. Communicate corporate direction clearly to all employees.
3. Have clear goals and objectives.
4. Set goals as a combination of top-down and bottom-up involvement.
5. Listen to employees.
6. Create a safe environment where employees can deliver bad news without the fear of criticism, being perceived as a poor team player, or termination.
7. Obtain lots of suggestions from employees.
8. Consult employees before making decisions that impact them.

9. Focus on results rather than methods or activities.

10. Delegate results, not tasks.

11. Encourage risk, mistakes, and failure as tools for learning and improving.

12. Refrain from micromanaging employees' actions and decisions.

How empowered are your employees? One of best ways to determine this is to observe their behavior. Do they behave the same or differently when:

- Their manager is out of town versus in town?
- They work alone versus part of a team?
- They are being observed or left up to their own devices?
- It is near their review time or after a review?
- They are a new employee rather than a seasoned veteran?
- They are in a support role or a management one?

If your employees never make mistakes, you may not have an empowered environment. If your employees never take risks or communicate reality, be advised: you may have a heavy, top-down 1960s-style management culture. And if you do, you may be in serious trouble. The world may be passing you by without you even knowing it.

The thing always happens that you really believe in; and the belief in a thing makes it happen.

—FRANK LLOYD WRIGHT

CHALLENGE #43: *Fostering a Fun and Rewarding Culture and Environment*

Several years ago, I worked with a client in the Midwest. One day during lunch, several of the employees were playing Frisbee out behind the plant. The president came out and asked what they were doing. One of the employees said, "We are on our lunch break, and we are playing." The president replied, "This is a place of business, not a playground. You are here to work, not have fun." I couldn't believe my ears. I can tell you that I have never before or since heard such a ridiculous remark from the president of a major business entity.

So, you say, what's the big deal? Some of you may believe that the president was right in his attitude. But I can only tell you that when people work in a fun environment (and I don't mean playing Frisbee in the halls), they:

- Will be more productive
- Will make fewer mistakes
- Will release their stress in a productive way rather than on a customer or fellow employee
- Will get along better with everyone
- Will come in early and leave late and not be driven by the clock, but by the project, assignment, or task
- Will tend to have more organizational loyalty
- Will give you the labor of their hearts—not just their hands

The opposite is going to be true in an environment filled with mistrust, disrespect, stress, politics, game-playing, and heavy top-down policies. In a labor market where good people can be hard to find, it makes sense to treat employees as your most valuable asset. That is because today, employees generally:

- Are smarter
- Have more options
- Don't need you or your job as much as you think they do
- Want to be respected, trusted, and accepted

How would you describe your organizational environment? Is it a fun place to work? Do employees look forward to Monday or just Friday? Have you ever asked them? You really don't have to. Their performance, attitudes, productivity, communication styles, creativity, willingness to take responsibility, morale, and results are (or will be) a pretty accurate barometer.

Nothing is so contagious as enthusiasm. It moves stones, it charms brutes. It is the genius of sincerity, and truth accomplishes no victories without it.

—EDWARD BULWER-LYTTON

CHALLENGE #44: *Holding People Accountable*

One of the major challenges facing organizations today is ensuring accountability with its policies, procedures, and philosophy. And I have seen numerous instances in which rules, standards, expectations, and policies within a company are continuously ignored, sabotaged, or broken.

As a manager, business owner, or executive, ensuring that what you *expect* to happen is *actually* happening on a routine basis is often a difficult, yet necessary, task. Lack of accountability will be the norm where one or more of these factors are present: favored employees, ego-centered management styles, inconsistent discipline for infractions, expecting behavior without taking the time or effort to inspect that the behavior is actually happening, or out-of-control management arrogance.

You can't manage any part of your organization from behind your desk. You must circulate, be visible, and get to know your people. This takes commitment and time, but I guarantee it will pay positive dividends in the long run.

Perceptions become reality in the minds of employees. It doesn't matter if what they believe is true or not. If they believe it is true in their minds, then it is as good as true, and they will behave accordingly.

One of the best ways to determine the prevailing perceptions and attitudes throughout your organization is to conduct an employee perception and attitude audit. To be truly accurate and effective, I recommend you retain an outside organization to conduct it. It should also be confidential.

The employees must feel free to share reality without the fear of retribution or punishment for delivering bad news.

There are three premises for your consideration when it comes to accountability:

1. Expecting different results from repeated behavior is a mild form of insanity.

2. You get the behavior you reward in your organization. If you want to change behavior, you must change the reward system that is in place.

3. All culture flows top-down. You can't change an organization from the bottom-up. Until you have clarified, unified, delivered, and reinforced a clear top-down focus, you will tend to get inconsistency in employee performance and productivity.

People have a way of becoming what you encourage them to be— not what you nag them to be.

—S.N. PARKER

CHALLENGE #45: *Rewarding the Right Behavior*

Behavior reinforced and rewarded is behavior repeated. This simple yet profound concept is at the root of more poor productivity, broken relationships, negative personnel issues, and high costs of doing business than any other management principle.

What does getting the behavior you reward mean? Let me give you an example. You want an employee who is always late to be on time. But you don't bring up their tardiness to them because it is only ten minutes. So there you sit with frustration, wishing and hoping the person would just get the message and be on time. The rule here is: be on time. But, unfortunately they don't get it (or choose not to), and your unspoken reaction will tend to reinforce their current behavior, so they continue to be late. By not addressing their lateness with them, you are sending the message that being late is acceptable. It also sends a message to other employees, who are on time but might want to be late once in a while, that being late is OK. No consequences.

There are hundreds, no thousands, of ways that managers reward the behavior they don't want and then seem surprised that they get more of it. What behavior are you rewarding in your organization that you need to change? Look at the behavior you want discontinued, and then determine why that particular person is acting in that way. If you don't like the behavior, you need to change the reward system. I am not just talking here about financial rewards, but social, physical, and so on.

How do you meet this challenge? The first step in changing behavior is to recognize the behavior that you would like changed. The next is to evaluate the reward system—why they are acting that way. Finally, look at your own behavior and how you are contributing to their actions. This is not an easy task, but one that will pay handsome dividends in productivity, improved morale, improved communication, and a better bottom line.

CHALLENGE #46: *Maintaining a* What *instead of a* Who *Corporate Culture*

You are a new employee and during your first week you notice that one of the procedures in your department, if updated, would greatly improve overall department productivity. You have an idea that would solve this productivity issue, so—since your organization has an open-door policy—you decide to bring your idea to the attention of the manager. Her reaction is appreciative, but in no uncertain terms she tells you that "this is the way we do things here, and since you are a new employee, it's understandable that you would not yet be aware of the rationale for this procedure."

Two hours later, your fellow employee who has been at the company for years, walks into your manager's office wanting to discuss the same problem you had just informed her about. He has a solution that is the same as the one you brought to her earlier, that he came up with independently. (He isn't trying to undercut you in any way.) The manager says to him, "Thanks for bringing this issue to my attention; let's implement your idea immediately."

This is a *Who* organization. The manager's behavior wasn't about what was best for the health and success of the organization; it was about *who* had the ideas or solutions or delivered a message.

In a *What* organization, it doesn't matter what your position, experience, tenure, or political clout is. None of this matters. The only thing that is important is *what* is best for the future success and health of this organization. I can tell you that What organizations tend to be the most successful over time, and Who organizations tend to have ongoing morale, communication, turnover, and productivity problems.

Is your organization a Who or What organization? Are you a Who or a What manager? How can you tell? Challenge yourself to implement the following actions of a What culture:

1. Give everyone in the organization the respect they deserve regardless of their position, roles, or responsibilities.
2. Listen actively to everyone, no matter what their employee circumstances or tenure.
3. If you have an open-door policy, ensure that when people come through it, you have an open mind.
4. Eliminate personal agendas you may have toward certain employees or departments.
5. Refrain from patronizing an employee who brings you an idea or makes a suggestion—no matter how good or bad the idea may be. Maybe their next one could be a real winner for your organization. But if you make them feel "what's the point?" they won't bring the next one to you, and you all lose.
6. Validate employees constantly. Read my book, *Nit-pickers, Naggers, and Tyrants.*
7. Follow through with employees who make a suggestion or recommendation, regardless of whether the idea or suggestion is implemented or not.
8. Keep in mind the simple premise: you get the behavior you reward.

9. Encourage bottom-up feedback of ideas, problems, information, and reality.
10. Try an anonymous survey. Ask your employees one question: are we a Who or What organization? Obviously you will need to explain what you mean by this. This is a chance to get everyone on the same page.

The sun and moon shine on all without partiality.

—CONFUCIUS

CHALLENGE #47: *Being an Encourager*

Today, more than ever, employees need to feel worthwhile. Due to the tremendous changes that are occurring in Corporate America, many employees feel greater levels of stress, overload, time pressure, and that—no matter what they do—it's never good enough or fast enough.

No wonder morale in many organizations is at an all-time low. No wonder employee turnover is a serious problem for so many employers. No wonder poor productivity is a critical concern for so many managers.

One of the best ways to ensure that your employees feel validated, worthwhile, and valuable is to take the time and energy to encourage them. Many managers are too stressed out and too busy to take the time for this vital activity. Many of them feel that employees get their positive feedback each week in a paycheck, and that should be enough. Sorry, folks, it isn't.

It is easy—with shrinking sales or margins, mergers and acquisitions, growth, and any number of other corporate issues—to not find the time or energy to send an encouraging message to an employee. Why not rise to this challenge though and take some time today to send a letter to the supervisor of someone who provided you with excellent service, or give just a friendly smile and a kind word about what a super job they did for you. It will make their day. Form the habit of sending at least two or three brief notes a day (even a post card) to someone, telling them that you appreciate them and how special they are, or to acknowledge what they did for you.

There are so many ways just to say thanks, I appreciate you, you can do it, you are fantastic, or whatever to your employees or the employees of your customers or suppliers. You will be amazed at the results. You will make their day. And you will feel better in the process. What a win-win situation!

CHALLENGE #48: *Creating a Motivating Climate and Culture*

If an employee lacks motivation, why is it your job to motivate them? A fundamental premise of motivation is this: the job of a manager is not to motivate their employees, but to create a motivating climate and culture where employees are willing and able to maintain a high degree of self-motivation.

You are responsible to people, but not for them. The job of a manager is "to manage," which implies achieving results through people. If you have to spend a great deal of your time worrying about why certain employees are not motivated or figuring out how to keep them motivated, I guarantee you that you will be spending a lot less time on some of your more important roles and responsibilities.

Instead of the fear or incentive tactics discussed earlier, why not spend your time creating a positive and motivating climate and culture and letting the chips fall where they may?

Those employees who lack the ability to stay motivated will sooner or later weed themselves out of your organization. Those who have the self-motivation capabilities will not require as much of your time or energy, allowing you to focus on more important tasks.

Often employees who lack self-motivation are only looking for attention, validation, or special consideration. Remember, you get the behavior you reward, so if you give these poorly motivated employees more time and attention—to keep them motivated—than you do to your motivated employees, what's the subtle message you are sending to your motivated employees?

Spend your time with your new hires and superstars and stop wasting time on your falling stars. In the long run, they are not going to make your job easier or your desired results more attainable, and I guarantee that, sooner rather than later, they will quit or need to be terminated. Look at all of that wasted time and energy that could have been directed elsewhere.

CHALLENGE #49: *Rewarding Performance rather than Tenure or Position*

One of the major themes of this book is this: you get the behavior you reward. This is an especially significant challenge when you are dealing with less-than-productive, long-term employees.

I am not implying that all of your long-term employees are in this category. But if your compensation program, management style, and culture are rewarding tenure instead of performance, I guarantee that having a lot of longer-term employees means you are less competitive, successful, or profitable in the marketplace than you would like to be.

Many organizations have a bonus program where everyone shares equally at the end of a quarter or year, depending on organizational performance. The problem with this approach is that in any group of employees, there will always be some that are more productive and others that are less productive. Yet, if everyone shares equally in a bonus of any kind, you are sending the message that it doesn't matter how effective you are, how hard you work, or whether you obey the rules or policies or not. None of that matters. In the end, everyone is rewarded equally just for showing up.

This process sends a loud and clear message to your better employees: why bother?!

Compensation is only one way that older, more senior, or longer-term employees are rewarded. There are special awards, banquets, special privileges, certain perks, and so on. I am not saying I am against these. I do, however, feel that if you use them or integrate them into your management style or corporate culture exclusively, there will be some negative consequences.

What you get by reaching your destination is not nearly as important as what you will become by reaching it.

—DR. ROBERT ANTHONY

CHALLENGE #50: *Maintaining a Safe Corporate Culture*

If employees are holding back or modifying the information they are giving to customers or management because it may not be safe for them to be honest, I guarantee that sooner or later this misinformation will lead to poor decisions and confused and lost customers, and will ultimately cost you sales and growth.

What is an unsafe emotional corporate environment? What can cause or contribute to an unsafe emotional environment?

Answer me this: if every time your employees open their mouths, you judge, criticize, invalidate, interrupt, or don't listen to them, how much do you think they will share further information, ideas, solutions, or departmental realities with you? You guessed it. Nil. Without a safe culture or environment, it is impossible for you as a manager to be in touch with the reality of what is going on in your department or organization. What causes this is a management style that is arrogant, insecure, invalidating, ego-driven, or power-hungry.

What are the consequences of having an unsafe corporate culture? Here are just a few to start your thinking:

- A we-and-they culture
- A lack of creative solutions to problems
- Poor communication
- Low morale
- Lots of rumor and hearsay
- High turnover of personnel
- Less-than-satisfied customers

What can you do to change it?
- Become an empathetic listener
- Value, respect, and trust your employees
- Lock your ego in the closet—or, better yet, harness it to serve you and others

A safe corporate culture is one where truth is encouraged bottom-up and top-down regardless of its acceptance or comfort. Insecure managers don't want bad news. They see it as whining or complaining. Good managers want reality— truth—regardless of who or what is responsible for a problem, failure, or mistake—even if it was them. Customers want truth also. "Don't tell me it will be delivered next week when you know it could be three-to-four weeks."

Keep away from people who try to belittle your ambitions. Small people always do that, but the really great make you feel that you, too, can become great.

—MARK TWAIN

CHALLENGE #51: *Getting Ownership to Projects and Goals*

If a new initiative, project, or program is to be successful, it will require the participation, support, and ownership of any number of employees in different departments or disciplines. Failure to achieve employee ownership will guarantee that your initiatives will achieve less than stellar results.

Achieving a high level of employee commitment and ownership requires a number of attitudes, behaviors, and skills. Here are a few to consider:

1. Believe that the program or initiative will be a success from the start.
2. Include employees in the discussions prior to its launch.
3. Encourage and validate their ideas, solutions, and contributions.
4. Encourage a discussion of challenges, problems, and real-world issues.
5. Allocate adequate resources to the program, decision, or project.
6. Establish benchmarks and goal evaluation points.
7. Give authority with responsibility.
8. Be willing to let go of the control of the program once it has begun.
9. Appoint a program champion who will take charge of its follow-through.
10. Refuse to quit at the first sign of failure or malfunction.
11. Encourage continuous upward feedback of reality.
12. Measure your progress from the beginning.
13. Reward active participation.

No project, program, or initiative is a sure winner from the beginning. Vigilance, patience, on-going belief, and continuous re-evaluation are required to ensure a successful outcome. Occasionally you must also let go of a project when it becomes clear that it was not consistent with your mission, objectives, or goals.

Motivation is what gets you started.
Habit is what keeps you going.

—JIM RYUN

CHAPTER 8

COACHING CHALLENGES

There is a difference between training and coaching. Training is teaching people what to do, when to do it, and how to do it. (That's the next chapter.) Coaching is catching people doing it right or wrong and guiding them either to do it better or to do it right. Coaching is a gradual modification of behavior by rewarding the behavior you want continued and bringing incorrect or inappropriate behavior or actions to the awareness of the individual so they can see how it needs to change. Remember, all discovery is self-discovery.

You cannot manage your organization from behind your desk. It is critical for coaching success that you circulate among your employees so you can observe behavior in action.

Coaching must be tailored to the background, experience, personality style, goals, skill level, and attitudes of the individual. To do otherwise is to invite frustration and failure.

Effective coaching should be done in private so as to preserve the self-image and status of the individual receiving the coaching among his or her peers. No one likes the disapproval of their fellow employees.

Effective coaching should build on existing strengths while attempting to change inappropriate actions. When coaching an individual, always affirm something positive or right that they are doing, before discussing the inappropriate behavior.

Annual reviews are not an effective way to coach employees in the long term. You shouldn't wait a year or even six months to fix undesirable behavior. That is why coaching is so effective—it is positive, spontaneous, motivating, and productive.

There are two ways to have highly productive employees. Hire perfect employees (unlikely!) or coach employees into a higher level of performance. Coaching, as I have said, is a different activity than training and one that takes a great deal of time, observation, employee involvement, discussion, and patience. Coaching is just one form of feedback.

I mentioned earlier the old saying, "Don't send your ducks to eagle school." Not everyone was meant to fly as high as the eagles. I believe that everyone has unlimited potential, but I also believe that many people are unwilling to do their part to ensure that their potential is realized. Some people are satisfied flying closer to the ground. Some people need to soar. Neither behavior nor attitude is right or wrong. People have a right to their own objectives and lifestyle goals.

The objective of consistent, positive, and pertinent coaching is to help employees to want to do better, period. Coaching guides the employee, regardless of position, to the higher ground.

Company presidents often fail to give adequate coaching time to their vice presidents. Their assumption is that because vice presidents are paid a six-figure income and have twenty-five years of experience, they should be able to just jump in and do the job correctly all the time. Not so. They may not need coaching on Management 101, people skills, or the basics of the business, but they will need time with the president to be able to get up to speed on corporate history, rituals, perceptions, expectations, and historical issues that have impacted where the organization is today.

Managers often tell me they are too busy with paperwork, administrative issues, or meetings to coach their employees. That is why so many companies must resort to crisis management—when employees at whatever level, from the president to the janitor, keep repeating the same mistakes, ignoring the consequences of previous mistakes, or being oblivious to the fact that mistakes are being made. These mistakes, errors, or whatever you want to call them are costing your organization right off the bottom line. Coaching is one way to improve results by reducing mistakes.

There are also numerous benefits for hiring an outside coach. An outside coach:

- Will bring objectivity to the employees' actions and behaviors
- Doesn't have agendas with the employee or the organization
- Tends to be neutral in situations where the person's manager might get too emotionally involved

- Is not wrapped up in corporate politics and, therefore, can remain neutral in situations that involve potential conflict

There is a reason why Olympic athletes have coaches even though they are the world's best in their sport. They want to get better, and they need the experience, expertise, objectivity, and support of someone they respect and trust.

If you are not coaching all of your employees regularly, you are missing opportunities to help them help you and your organization excel.

First say to yourself what you would be; then do what you have to do.

—EPICTETUS

CHALLENGE #52: *Playing Fair at Checkers*

Maintaining some employees' high levels of motivation and performance is a challenge for many employers today. But sometimes it seems that it takes far too much energy to keep an employee highly motivated and performing well. Why? Perhaps they are not playing fair at checkers.

In the game of checkers, one of the basic rules is that one player cannot move his tokens until the other player moves one of hers. In other words, no one can move twice in a row unless, of course, they jump their opponent (which we call cheating). What does checkers have to with employee productivity and motivation?

I have been suggesting for years that management play a form of checkers with their employees. Let me explain, taking the hiring of a new employee as an example.

1. Your move: You interview the candidate. Their move: They present themselves professionally.
2. Your move: You offer them a position. Their move: They accept the position.
3. Your move: You offer them training and support. Their move: They take advantage of the training and use it.
4. Your move: You continue to give them the tools and support they need to be effective. Their move: They keep on learning and growing.

And so the game progresses. Here's the problem. If an employee doesn't move when it is his turn, two things can happen:

1. You move again for him (which is what many managers do today).
2. The game is over until he moves.

Why do many managers move twice? Why do they feel the need to move again when the employee does not move when it is his turn? Is it because they feel ultimately responsible for the employee's motivation or success? Or is it because they don't want to feel responsible for their employee's failure? Some managers avoid or can't handle confrontation in any form. And others simply don't know how to keep the game going as a win-win proposition for everyone.

I'll bet that at least 50 percent of the managers, executives, or business owners reading this chapter have at least one employee that has stopped moving, and the manager, feeling obliged to get the employee to move, moves twice in a row. (This is cheating, if you recall.) Some managers keep on moving indefinitely when the employee fails to move, until they get to the point when they finally realize the employee is never going to move, and the game has been over for months, or even years.

Three critical premises are at work here:
1. You get the behavior you reward.
2. You are responsible to people, but not for them.
3. Detachment—when you are concerned enough to be interested in employees and support them, but still recognize that their "stuff" is theirs to handle—is a positive move that keeps the game going; whereas disengage-

ment—when you no longer care or are interested—is a negative move.

Sometimes employees stop moving because their manager or their organization did not move when it was their turn. For example, let's say you are expecting your employees to pick up the extra workload caused by employees who have left the organization. You choose not to replace them, but to ask the remaining employees to do more: come in earlier, stay later, or take on more responsibility. But you haven't given them any more support, recognition, appreciation, or compensation. You are asking them to move, but you have failed to move by giving more to them. Remember, folks, this game goes both ways.

What will be the outcome of this approach? The manager doesn't move, so the employee loses her motivation— "Why bother?"—and the manager becomes stressed and frustrated because the employee has stopped moving. Either way, this environment is not conducive to peak performance and responsibility, but rather to finger-pointing and blame.

I ask you: are you improving your skills as a manager or are you about as good at checkers as you were twenty years ago?

The more honor and respect among the players, the greater the team.

—Unknown

CHALLENGE #53: *Having and Maintaining Consistent Standards*

Without clear, communicated, and understood standards or expectations, it is difficult for employees to know what to do, when to do it, and how to do it. It is difficult for managers as well, as they must ensure that their expectations are being satisfied. If standards vary according to the whims of management, the ebb and flow of the economy, competitors' philosophies, changes in government rules or laws, or the fickleness of consumers, then profits, productivity, and market share will surely be at variance with the expectations of management.

Let me share a real example in which performance suffered and coaching became nothing more than a waste of time and energy due to inconsistent standards, rules, or expectations. Several years ago I worked with a company that was having difficulty maintaining morale and motivation among the majority of its employees. After interviewing a number of employees, I discovered that the major problem was inconsistency in terms of expectations. The degree of performance expectations was determined not by employees' ability or tenure but by whether or not they were in the "favored status" of management.

Some employees were disciplined for certain behaviors while others who exhibited those same behaviors were exempt from any negative feedback. When the managers of the employees who were not "favored" attempted to coach these employees toward better performance, you can easily guess the employees' reaction. Suffice it to say, these employees' coaching was all but useless.

To paraphrase the late W. Edwards Deming, the great management guru: If standards and expectations are clear, then even people with less than ideal talent will tend to succeed. The purpose of coaching is to help employees achieve measurable performance-based behavior. If the performance standards vary, you will find that you may become a fraud when attempting to coach those employees who have the potential, but just don't fit into one of your special employee categories. Saying to an employee that the policy is to be on time and take one-hour lunches—meanwhile, two or three of your other employees consistently wander into the office after two-hour lunches—makes you look like a fool or a liar or both.

Certainly, standards, policies, and procedures must change to reflect the current state of the economy, your organization's market position, or the needs and desires of your customers. But you must maintain and use consistent standards to support your coaching and, ultimately, attain success.

Look to make your course regular, that men may know beforehand what they may expect.

—FRANCIS BACON

CHAPTER 9

TRAINING CHALLENGES

For years, I have observed an interesting phenomenon in Corporate America. Many organizations invest thousands, and often millions, of dollars each year on new equipment, office furniture, advertising, promotion campaigns, and any number of investments that they hope will improve their sales, profits, customer satisfaction levels, amount of repeat business, or ability to beat the competition. However, they spend very little on developing the employees who will use the equipment, deal with the customers, and attempt to sell against the competition. For example, the importance of effective customer service is being given a lot of lip service these days. Yet in the recent past, I have had no fewer than a dozen negative experiences with organizations who tout "We Care" on name badges, signs on the walls, or in their advertising and marketing literature. The words are there, but apparently the employees whom I dealt with were on vacation when the program was initiated.

Customer-service training is not a cost, but an investment in repeat business. Sales training is not a cost, but an investment in a more profitable business. Management training is not a cost, but insurance that your employees and your organization are primed for the future in a positive way.

The average manager today who is responsible for the performance, motivation, and productivity of any number of employees lacks the necessary management skills and people skills to be effective. Period.

The solution is not sending people to a half-day seminar. Although this is better than doing nothing, it isn't much better. The retention of new information covered in a half- or full-day seminar is one to two weeks at best. You don't change behavior that an employee has developed over years of early conditioning and reinforcement in just three hours. You change it by reinforcement, consistency, and accountability over time. Are these three factors of employee training present in your organization?

CHALLENGE #54: *Investing in Employee Development*

Corporate America is undergoing rapid and dynamic cultural changes. Corporate downsizing, restructuring, and reorganization have employees running scared and under a great deal of stress. These issues are having a dramatic impact on employee productivity, morale, and communication patterns throughout every organization that has been touched in some way by advancing technology, increased competition, globalization, and a redefined mission and purpose.

Employees are being asked to do more, take on more responsibility, work longer hours, work harder, take work home—often with fewer supporting systems and less structure. This environment is playing havoc with margins, sales, and profits for many organizations. It is unlikely that your organization has gone untouched by some or all of these factors. One of the most effective ways you can counter these issues is through better training and retraining of every employee in your organization, from the president or CEO down to the cook, drivers, janitors, and everyone in between. Employee development in today's competitive world is no longer a luxury. Employees need constant training and reinforcement of skills and attitudes to ensure an effective and profitable organization.

Training and employee development are some of the best ways to ensure improved sales, profits, and market share. Poorly trained employees often want to be more effective but just don't know how. When you give employees the tools they need to be effective—through training—you help them, but you also help yourself and your organization.

Picking out one segment of your business for training—like the customer service staff or sales group—and ignoring your management team is flirting with disaster. I have observed dramatic success when every employee is developed, and I have witnessed failure, management frustration, vulnerability to competition, and reduced market share and customer loyalty when organizations select only special groups, individuals, and/or departments for training. Everyone in your organization is a profit center, either directly or indirectly. Everyone, sooner or later, touches a customer in some way. Every employee can be a positive influence for growth or a cause of lost business, lagging profits, excessive sales costs, or wasted corporate resources. To think otherwise is to be naive. Some managers see spending on training as a cost rather than an investment in a secure future. How short-sighted!

Training has many benefits. Here are just a few:

1. It can improve employee loyalty.
2. It can improve employee morale.
3. It can reduce employee turnover.
4. It can reduce sales costs.
5. It can improve organizational effectiveness.
6. It can reduce hiring costs and time.
7. It can improve organizational communication.
8. It can competitor-proof your business.
9. It can improve customer loyalty.
10. It can improve profits.

That should be enough to convince you that investing in your employees is one of the best decisions you can make over the long haul.

I find the great thing in this world is not so much where we stand, as in what direction we are moving.

— OLIVER WENDELL HOLMES, JR.

CHALLENGE #55: *Seeing Training as an Investment rather than a Cost*

During the years, many of my clients have chosen to see devoting time and money toward training their people as an investment and not as a cost. Others have cut back on training when the economy was spiraling out of control. Their rationale was: "cut back now: we can invest in our employees when there is more cash available."

Training is a cost:

1. When it is done poorly
2. When it is done too late
3. When too little is done
4. When it doesn't touch everyone
5. When it is not reinforced
6. When it doesn't relate to where you are headed

Training is an investment:

1. Because it tells your people you care about them.
2. Because your only source of revenue is your people. Yes, yes, I know. You need trucks, equipment, computers and pencils—but in the long run, it is your people who make effective use of all of these capital expenditures.
3. Because your people touch your customers every day. What messages are they sending as they sell to them, collect from them, or service them?
4. Because there are two ways to improve the bottom line: (1) generate more income and (2) reduce redundant, wasteful costs. Your people are responsible for both.

I could go on, but I would like to leave you with a simple question. Are you a smart manager who sees training as an investment in your present and future success?

CHALLENGE #56: *Using Outside Resources for Training*

I have a simple rule when it comes to developing your employees' skills and attitudes. Use inside staff for the specific skills and go outside the organization for the generic skills. Specific skills refer to the particular job skills, such as the administrative, technical, manufacturing, distribution, and finance abilities employees need to do their jobs. The generic skills are areas such as sales, customer service, management, communication, and motivation training that employees need to ensure that their job skills are put to good use.

I have often been asked why I believe in this approach. I have worked with hundreds of organizations in a number of industries. I know nothing about how to develop software, build jets, manufacture tuxedos, or research pharmaceuticals. These skills are best left to inside people who have the talent, experience, and know-how to teach others these abilities.

So, why not let inside staff also train people on sales or management skills as well? Keep in mind, I am not referring to those unique sales skills that are particular to your products or industry. What I am referring to is the ability to sell, manage, or handle customer issues.

Using inside staff for these disciplines will often cause more problems than they solve. Let me give you two examples.

Let's say you have a training department, and after extensive organization research, the department comes to the conclusion that senior management is in dire need of improved people skills or leadership ability. They put together a training program to address these needs and then inform the CEO, CFO, chief operating officer (COO), and president that they need to attend sessions on these topics. Do you really think that the trainers will get into specific sensitive issues that are being caused by these folks' management styles? I seriously doubt that will happen or that much will be accomplished. A competent individual from outside the company, however—who has no hidden agenda and is not involved in corporate politics or subject to termination—can be far more effective in delivering bad news and practical truths in a way that will allow change to happen without people in the company getting defensive.

Let's say that you promote a salesperson who is a great closer, but not good at customer follow-up. This person is given the role of teaching all of the sales staff how to increase sales. Here's what will happen. This individual will tend to pass on her strengths as well as her weaknesses during this training. In other words, she will create great closers who fall short of effective customer-relationship skills. The reason is that she will be far more comfortable teaching what she is good at and will tend to avoid those topics where she is weak. An outside trainer, however, will bring value in all of the needed sales skills and will not avoid certain topics or make judgments about what should be done and how.

We cannot solve our problems with the same level of thinking that created them.

—Albert Einstein

CHALLENGE #57: *Developing Curriculum-Based Training*

Your employees, regardless of their age, gender, experience, and education, have a variety of perceptions, agendas, self-esteem levels, objectives, values, and conditioned backgrounds. Combined, all of these generate a wide degree of behaviors, life outlooks, and attitudes. Many of these attitudes were formed very early in life as a result of a person's upbringing and their interpretation of their life experiences.

Now flash forward to the present. You want to get an employee or group of employees to change behavior in some way so as to improve effectiveness, productivity, sales ability, or communication patterns. So you put them through an extensive training program of some kind. They sit there for two or three days absorbing a variety of concepts, principles, or techniques that, when understood, embraced, and applied, will improve their performance and results.

Here's the problem: the average retention of a new idea is less than 15 percent after two weeks. Generally speaking, when you throw a plethora of information at employees in a condensed period of time, you are wasting their time and your money. This is because:

1. Unless the training is very specific to their roles or job functions, people generally go into a passive learning mode and do not to absorb or relate all of this information to their current circumstances.

2. Since the average retention is very low after only several days, you often will not see long-term change.

3. Individuals' values have been entrenched over a long period of time, and it is difficult to change these with only a one-time exposure to new ideas, philosophies, or concepts.

4. Often, the older people are, the less willing they are to embrace new ideas even though this new information may be of great value to them, their careers, or their lives.

5. Everyone has a unique learning style. Some learn best by hearing, others by seeing, and still others by doing. To put everyone in the same learning environment and assume that they will all "get it" is to be out of touch with a critical learning research.

As you can see, this "one-time" training approach has long-term limitations. The only solution to effectively changing individuals' behavior is to understand their learning styles, personal agendas, and needs, and then create unique learning opportunities for each employee. Yes, this can be more expensive in the beginning, but it will pay handsome dividends over the long haul. I am talking here about developing curriculum-based learning rather than one-shot learning as your employee-development philosophy.

Years ago as a trainer, I came to the conclusion that most people can change, but few are willing to do the work necessary to do so. This being the case, to put a group of employees in a room, hire an expensive speaker, and then assume that the trainees will leave the room better qualified immediately, is to risk frustration, stress, and a great deal of anxiety.

A better solution is to approach training the same way a high school algebra teacher does. That is, to give routine doses of new information, review, application, evaluation, and assignments or homework. There is no guarantee that everyone is going to master the skills with this approach, but your chances are greatly improved with this approach rather than the single-shot philosophy.

One learns by doing a thing; for though you think you know it, you have no certainty until you try.

—SOPHOCLES

CHALLENGE #58: *Inspecting the Training for Positive Outcomes*

One of the biggest challenges facing managers who invest money in training for their employees is developing reinforcement and integration strategies as well as accountability and measurement tools to ensure long-term results. I was once asked by a client if I would guarantee the outcome and use of the techniques, skills, and attitudes covered during my program. My response was "Yes, if you make me president."

The truth is, if it isn't being measured, it most likely isn't happening. If you want to ensure that the investment you make in money and your employees' time pays off, it is absolutely critical that you have a reinforcement strategy in place before you begin the training. If you fail to inspect or hold people accountable, you are sending employees the message that it really isn't necessary to get anything out of your training.

There are numerous ways to reinforce and inspect. Here are just a few:

1. Hold weekly training-review meetings on the material covered and ask people to give you real-world examples of how they are applying what they learned.

2. Give them books to read or CDs to listen to after the completion of the training and ask them to give you reports—not just of the material covered, but on what they learned and how they plan to use it.

3. Create a buddy system. Assign two people to work together for several weeks after the training. Their responsibility is to hold each other accountable.

4. Ask them to teach a portion of what they have learned to others in their department or group.
5. Give them a quiz or test several weeks after the training to see what they remember and are still using. (I often supply these to my clients for their use.)

CHAPTER 10

LEADERSHIP CHALLENGES

One of the biggest challenges managers face today—from the senior level on down—is communicating corporate direction with clarity and consistency to all employees who have a right and need to know. Most organizations do a poor job of this at best.

From boardrooms to lunchrooms across America, the discussions are almost always the same. In the lunchrooms the question is, "Who are we and where are we going?" In the boardrooms, the question is "Where are we going and how do we get there?"

In either case, the consequences are the same, what I call "Direction Drift." It is a critical challenge facing Corporate America today. The consequences of direction drift are many, but they can be summarized into just five:

1. A lack of communicated direction contributes to poor employee performance and productivity.
2. A lack of clear direction increases the likelihood of wasted corporate resources.

3. A lack of focused direction adds a negative element to corporate culture, mainly the "here we go again" syndrome.

4. A lack of consistent direction adds a great deal of uncertainty to the attitudes of employees whose primary function is to take the organization where it is headed.

5. A lack of confident direction is a signal to employees, the marketplace, and your competitors that you are vulnerable and unsure of your objectives and strategies.

What is the cause of this malaise? I believe there are five distinct contributors to this problem:

1. Senior management is not in touch with the reality of either the organization or the marketplace—or both.

2. Senior management is stuck in an historical perspective and is unable or unwilling to revisit its role and fundamental purpose as a business entity.

3. Change is coming so fast and furious that organizations are unable or unwilling to develop a correct perspective on what is really happening in the world, whether their "world" is regional or the international arena.

4. Arrogance or ignorance prevents management from admitting that it needs to rewrite the company's mission statement, philosophy, approaches, strategies, core values, or plans.

5. Inaction seems safer than wrong action.

The world is not going to sit idly by as organizations wait for a sure and safe path into the future to become evident.

Somewhere in the world today, some organization is zeroing in on your customers and your market position. You can ill afford to continue to adhere to a "wait and see" philosophy. Boldness, responsiveness, clear vision, flexibility, fast response time, and courage will be the benchmarks of future successful organizations.

There are three areas that I encourage you to consider if you want to be on the leading edge in the coming years:

1. You must put in place a system of open, honest, top-down, and bottom-up communication.
2. You must tap the resources of your most valuable asset, your people.
3. You must do more than listen to your customers; you must think ahead of them and offer them what they will want in the future, not what you want to give them because it is convenient, cost-effective, or within the current scope of your strategy.

There are any number of approaches and philosophies available to executives today, from Total Quality Management to Principle-Centered Leadership. They will all help you if you are not clear on your direction and objectives. Any one of them can propel you with lightning speed into the future—if you know where you are going and why.

CHALLENGE #59: *Defining and Personalizing Your Leadership Style*

According to James MacGregor Burns, who authored the Pulitzer Prize–winning book *Leadership*, there are at least 130 current definitions of leadership. Warren Bemis and Burt Nanus, in their book *Leaders*, claim there are at least 350. Here are a few:

1. We have conceived of leadership as leaders tapping into the existence, potential motive, and power basis of followers, for the purpose of achieving an intended change.

2. Though leadership may be hard to define, the one characteristic common to all leaders is their ability to make things happen.

3. Leadership is the will to control events, the understanding to chart a course, and the power to get a job done, cooperatively using the skill and abilities of other people.

4. Leadership is the ability to get men and women to do what they don't want to do and like it.

5. Leadership appears to be the art of getting others to want to do something you are convinced should be done.

Here are the most frequently mentioned leadership traits (not in any particular order):

- Courage
- Optimism
- Sense of duty
- Vision for the future (for self and others)

- Unbending character
- Strong faith
- Integrity
- Purpose
- Compassion
- Realism
- Action
- Work ethic
- Spirituality
- Competence
- Charisma
- Effort
- Service to others
- Self-discipline
- Moral excellence
- Ability to handle power, success, and failure
- Influence
- Sense of humor
- Charity
- Humility
- A learning attitude
- Endurance
- A builder of people and enterprise
- Respect for others, life, and principles
- Personality
- People skills
- Handling uncertainty
- An ability to control emotions
- Positive-change agent

- Ability to foster trust
- Making difficult decisions

I doubt you would find them all in any single person. So the questions for consideration are:

1. Which ones are absolutely required in every leader?
2. Which ones would be nice to have, but are not vital for effective leadership?
3. Which ones turn up the least in the average good leader?
4. Which single trait is critical if none of the others are present?

The way you answer will indicate your own preference for leadership style.

The new leadership paradigm

A number of clients have asked me what I believe is the difference between leadership of the past and what it will take to maintain a leadership position in the future. Here are my thoughts:

The leadership paradigm of the past was based on:	The leadership paradigm of the future will be based on:
• Mistrust	• High Trust
• Fear/Incentives	• Empowerment
• Selection	• Open Communication
• Communication	• Inclusion
• Exclusion	• Team Approach
• Single Business Units	• Individual Accountability
• Organization	• Work Is Fun
• Performance	• Bottom-Up Decisions
• Work Is Work	• Everyone Is Unique
• Top-Down Decisions	• Change Is to Be Embraced
• Everyone Is the Same	• Employee Freedom
• Change Is to Be Avoided	• Positive Reinforcement
• Employee Restrictions	• Mistakes Are Good
• Negative Reinforcement	
• Mistakes Are Bad	

What do you think?

CHALLENGE #60: *Making Consistently Good Decisions*

One of the most critical management traits is the ability to make sound decisions in a timely manner and to empower employees to do likewise. The ability to drive decision-making down the corporate ladder requires trust, confidence in employees, and a safe corporate culture. The following will give you some guidelines for your decision-making and the ability to empower others to make decisions. To make consistently good decisions:

1. Define the problem in writing.
2. Get as much information as you can—especially from the people who will be most affected by the decision.
3. Do not go into information overload.
4. Recognize that you will never have all of the information you need or want.
5. Get your information from several sources and not just people who will agree with you or validate you. Bypass your direct reports for some of this information.
6. Consider all of your possible alternatives, whether you are comfortable with them or not.
7. Evaluate all of the possible outcomes for each alternative. Think the decision through. Who will it impact? Now? Later? What could that impact be? What are the possible consequences of doing nothing?
8. Consider all of the potential and known and potentially unknown challenges, problems, resources, or threats. This takes experience and judgment.
9. Make the decision.

10. Communicate the decision to everyone who will either be impacted by it or who needs to be involved in supporting or integrating it.
11. Evaluate the consequences of the decision as they unfold.
12. Be willing to change the decision or take a few steps back as soon as you feel or believe that your decision is not working. One of the biggest mistakes is to stick with a bad decision long after it should have been stopped.
13. If the decision is not working, reevaluate by going back and repeating steps one through twelve.
14. Start a decision journal of the outcomes of previous decisions.
15. Remember: a decision to do nothing is still a decision.
16. Trust yourself and your insight, experience, and ability.
17. Look for the critical decision factors that are consistent with your strategy, vision, mission, and core values.

Personal leadership is the process of keeping your vision and values before you and aligning your life to be congruent with them.

—STEPHEN R. COVEY

CHALLENGE #61: *Sharing the Wealth*

Over the years, I have observed two distinct attitudes regarding "sharing the wealth" with employees. One attitude is that employees are paid to work, and when they do, they get to keep their jobs and get a check every week. The other attitude is that employees are valuable assets to the organization and contribute to its health, success, reputation, profitability, and performance. Managers who believe this tend to share the rewards with their employees.

While there are advantages and disadvantages to each of these philosophies, I would like to illustrate the major difference between the two—keeping the wealth among a select few or sharing the wealth with employees—using a "real-life" example from one of my previous clients.

The two owners of the company loved to keep everything for themselves. Not only that, they would flaunt their purchases in front of their employees. They would park their new Mercedes cars by the door so everyone could see them. They would talk incessantly about their latest toys. They would brag about how much money they made and what they could buy.

Meanwhile, their underpaid receptionist was unhappily using an original Windows computer that was too slow for her work and needed servicing. She was ready to quit.

Get my point? Understand that I am not against an owner or executive earning lots of money and buying whatever he or she wants. However, these two young owners had their priorities all wrong. If you keep it for yourself—fine, but don't act surprised at how your employees respond when they haven't had a raise in three years or must use worn-out equipment or cheap supplies.

So, how can smart managers and leaders share the wealth with their employees? Consider some different compensation systems:

1. Everyone can share in a bonus system—regardless of performance or contribution.
2. Only certain people (such as owners, management, certain peak performers, or family members) get to see any of this cash.
3. People receive bonuses based on their contribution to profitability or sales.
4. Everything left over goes to the owner or shareholders.

What is your attitude when it comes to sharing the wealth, and is it the best way to meet this particular challenge?

There is overwhelming evidence that the higher the level of self-esteem, the more likely one will be to treat others with respect, kindness, and generosity.

—NATHANIEL BRANDEN

CHALLENGE #62: *Following Your Own Rules even though You Are the Boss*

Too often supervisors, managers, executives, and business owners go to a great deal of trouble to establish policies, rules, and processes and then are the first to break them. Many feel that just because they are the "boss," they are entitled to do whatever they want. Yes, and no!

Here's an example of a family who owned a business with two hundred employees, about 20 percent of whom were in some way related to the owner. Family members, regardless of their position, came and went as they pleased over the course of each workday, with no consequences. Nonfamily employees were expected to follow the general rules, but the family members chose not to follow them. If a nonfamily employee took an hour and fifteen minutes for lunch, they were reprimanded; meanwhile, family members routinely took two-hour lunches.

Here's the point: when you have rules and not everyone is expected or required to adhere to them—because of position, tenure, or some other reason—you send a disastrous mixed message to all of your employees. I guarantee it will have a negative impact, sooner or later, on morale, turnover, and the respect employees have for management.

Just having the title of manager, president, or CFO does not give you the right to create organizational rules and then expect everyone but you to follow them. This is a tremendous insult to your employees and one that will have tremendous negative outcomes.

On the other hand, when you follow all of the rules—even the ones that your employees feel you are entitled to break because of your position—you send a message that everyone in your organization, regardless of position, tenure, or title is equal in all respects. This attitude, my friends, will foster tremendous respect, loyalty, and dedication by everyone who works for you.

CHALLENGE #63: *Maintaining Integrity at All Times*

Integrity and trust go hand-in-hand as qualities for success. It is not possible to have one without the other. If you trust someone, it is most likely because they are trustworthy: they have ethics or integrity. If a person lacks either of the two, they will generally lack both.

So, what is integrity? There are many people more expert than I who have written books, articles, and given speeches on this important topic. But let me give it my best shot here. Integrity is behaving as though you know that your every action, word, and thought—yes, your thoughts too—would be posted on the company bulletin board or the Internet for all to see.

It is the willingness and ability to do what *is* right—not what you *think* is right (and there is often a difference). Most people who have been brought up in the right surroundings know what is right, yet they hope they can get away with doing the wrong things and that their words and actions will remain forever locked in their own mind.

Sooner or later, we all get caught. We may not get caught in the way we were anticipating, but there is a law of cause and effect on this planet. Break the rules...pay the price, no matter where—in your health, relationships, or career.

The questions we must each ask ourselves when we consider doing what *is not* right versus what *is* are: Can I handle getting caught? Is the price worth it? How will I react to getting caught? Wouldn't it just be easier to deal in truth? All the time? The answer to the last two questions is, yes. So why do people misrepresent, lie, or tell little innocent fibs? To look good (or better than we are)? To protect themselves? To avoid conflict? I don't know. We are all guilty—at least one time in our lives or for most of us, several times—of shading the truth for what we feel is a justifiable cause. Is this wrong? I am not a moralist. But I do believe that character and integrity are related.

Challenge yourself with a few simple questions the next time you are considering anything less than truth:

1. What will I lose and gain by dealing in an untruth?
2. Who will this lack of truth impact other than me?
3. Is it easy for me to shade the truth, and do I do it often? Why?
4. If I deal only in the truth—all the time—what will that do for me?

Effective leadership is putting first things first. Effective management is discipline, carrying it out.

—Stephen R. Covey

CHALLENGE #64: *Staying in Touch with Reality*

Everything flows from the top down in an organization. Managers, leaders, and executives who point the finger elsewhere in their organization for the cause of its problems, challenges, mistakes, or negative issues are missing the boat. These people fail to realize that they are responsible for all of it: the good, the bad, and the ugly.

One way to find out what is really going on, what people really think, and what the real issues, needs, problems, opportunities, and challenges are, is to get out from behind your desk and circulate. Vow to spend at least one day a week just wandering through your organization, no matter whether it is a multinational corporation or a small business with only ten employees. Spend time with them, take them to lunch, listen to them, and observe. Keep your eyes and ears open and your mouth closed. Don't let your ego get in the way of some valuable research. Paying attention to bottom-up feelings, issues, and attitudes will prevent you from making serious misjudgments and poor decisions, and will end up saving you time, money, and resources.

Dare to answer the following questions for a better awareness of how your culture is impacting your organization's productivity, success, and bottom line:

1. Is the communication you receive being edited because of your position?
2. Are certain groups or departments more productive than others? Why?

3. What is the general direction of your organization's sales? Profits? Turnover?
4. How would you describe morale? Is it getting better? Worse? Remaining constant? How do you know? What barometers are you using?
5. What are the attitudes of the majority of your customers today? In the recent past?
6. Are people under a great deal of stress? Pressure? Are there shorter deadlines? Is there more work on their plates than they can finish in one lifetime?
7. Are you having difficulty keeping or attracting good employees?
8. Are your managers properly trained to get the greatest effectiveness from their employees?
9. What is your organizational culture?
10. Is your organizational philosophy hindering or contributing to your growth and success?
11. Is your management style getting you the long-term results you want?
12. What needs to change in your organization to achieve greater success?
13. Are you in touch with the reality of your situation?

On the Plains of Hesitation bleach the bones of countless millions, who, on the threshold of victory, sat down to wait, and in waiting, died.

—WILLIAM MARSTON

CHALLENGE #65: *Believing that Leadership Is Earned*

Leadership is not a title or an endowment. Leadership is earned. Leadership is the trust that employees have in their management to make good decisions that will have a positive, long-term impact on their careers and life. Employees follow leaders that inspire them to reach their full potential and the potential of their organizations. Effective leaders are more concerned with the success of their organization than they are with their own notoriety or fame. It is unfortunate, however, that many of today's leaders are more concerned with their own personal agendas, well-being, and success than those of their followers.

There are many ways to earn the right to lead. No single way is guaranteed to ensure employee loyalty or the success of an organization. The right to lead must be re-earned again and again as an enterprise grows and evolves through its many stages of development and transition. Leaders must continuously reinvent themselves with new skills, new knowledge, and new vision—for themselves and for their organizations.

It is also important to understand that leaders can be found at all levels of an organization and not just at the top. Leadership implies vision and a sense of how to improve in order to take advantage of emerging technology, methodologies, trends, and innovation in general. Leaders can be found on the shop floor and in a sales territory, in the customer service department, and in the lunchroom. Real leadership implies service to others and placing the needs of others above your own. Such leaders can be found throughout every organization, and they represent the future success of all organizations.

The first responsibility of a leader is to define reality. The last is to say thank you. In between, the leader is a servant.

—MAX DE PREE

CHALLENGE #66: *Making Change Your Partner*

There are numerous national and international organizations that are still being run by old school managers and executives. Many of these individuals are locked in a style of doing business that may have worked ten to twenty years ago—but times have changed since then. Many of these executives and managers are going to find themselves on the outside looking in and wondering how it happened, when it happened, and why it happened to them.

This is what I mean by old-school management style. See if the shoe fits for you.

1. Old-school managers or executives are top-down autocrats who give only lip service to bottom-up responsibility, decision-making, goal-setting, and problem-solving.
2. They are arrogant, closed-minded, and often aloof and inaccessible.
3. They believe to win means beating someone else.
4. They believe that other people in their organization shouldn't get too much recognition, compensation, responsibility, and/or freedom.
5. They believe that people should sacrifice their families, health, and personal agendas for the sake of the organization.
6. They are very competitive and would do anything to get a customer.
7. They are price- and profit-driven.
8. They use people up.
9. They often feel they are invincible.

10. They use threats, economic leverage, and fear to get results.

Now here is the paradigm of the future:
1. Smart and successful managers and executives listen to their employees, customers, and suppliers and work at creating partnerships both inside and outside the organization.
2. They empower people by pushing decision-making, authority, accountability, problem solving, goal setting, and risk taking down through the organization.
3. They create a strong team approach to projects, programs, objectives, and solving problems.
4. They encourage cooperation and open, honest communication.
5. They reward creativity, mistakes that contribute to improvements, and honest feedback.
6. They see change as an opportunity to grow.
7. They see problems as necessary to modify systems, strategies, policies, and procedures.
8. They are reflective, responsive, and accessible.
9. They are driven by creating quality of life for their employees, customers, and community.
10. They are generous with the fruits of their employees' labors.
11. They share openly and fairly.
12. They trust and believe in their people.
13. They are concerned about values, the environment, and relationships.

This is quite a contrast to old school managers, wouldn't you say? It should be an easy task to determine where you fit. You may not fall 100 percent into either group, but I'll bet you have more of one group's characteristics than the other. The challenge is that if you fall into the old-school category, it is time to look around you and notice that the world is changing. If you are in the progressive group, don't assume you have it made. Every day you will have your attitudes, values, expectations, and perceptions challenged. You are not home free yet. You must keep the vigil as you grow your organization, department, or division into the next decade and beyond. There will be plenty of new obstacles, challenges, and problems to test your resolve. So, relax and enjoy the roller coaster ride into the future.

Vision is the art of seeing things invisible.

—JONATHAN SWIFT

CHALLENGE #67: *Eliminating Sacred Cows*

Over the years, I have discovered that many organizations have a variety of policies, products, services, positions, techniques, and even people who are what I refer to as "sacred cows." In other words: don't mess with them. The people are protected because of their relationship to or with a certain manager or founder or because of their longevity with the company. Many policies, products, or services are the creation of a long-time manager or department and are untouchable.

I have not yet worked with or seen an organization that didn't have some sacred cows that need to be eliminated or redesigned. I'll bet if you look closely, you can find a few in your organization. The questions you need to ask are the following:

1. Is the current culture, internal environment, or business conditions driven by the sacred cows?

2. Do you have some people that need to be retrained with different skill sets?

3. Do you have positions or departments that are no longer necessary or relevant (for whatever reason)?

4. Are some policies outdated and getting in the way of employee performance and organization effectiveness?

5. Is it time to let go of a previous acquisition that it is no longer in your overall best interests to hang on to?

6. Are you considering an acquisition based solely on what your ego needs?

There are many issues to consider, of course. My objective here is to get you to take a fresh look at your organization as if you were a consultant who was charged with evaluating the overall performance of your organization and with making recommendations to improve overall performance and profitability. One of the best ways to accomplish this, other than bringing in an outsider (which is an excellent idea, by the way), is to ask your employees to give you honest feedback on behaviors, products, services, and policies that they feel are no longer current with the philosophy, goals, objectives, or mission of the organization.

If your culture is not based on honesty and safety, my guess is that you will not get real and accurate information, but will be told what your people think you want to hear. I suggest that you fix this first before you attempt to eliminate your sacred cows! Otherwise you are only kidding yourself.

Sacred cows make the best hamburger.

—Mark Twain

CHALLENGE #68: *Creating a Top-Down and Bottom-Up Organization*

Corporate, organizational, and departmental cultures all flow from the top down. The written and unwritten rules, policies, and philosophies of a manager or the organization all eventually find their way into the attitudes and performance of almost everyone in the organization. One of the critical things to remember when dealing with people is this: you get the behavior you reward. If the culture directly or indirectly rewards a certain type of attitude or behavior, you are, by your actions or inactions, probably reaffirming that these are acceptable. If you want to change behavior, you must first evaluate the culture that is in place that may be rewarding the type of behavior you are getting but don't necessarily want.

There are only three ways to manage your organization: top-down, bottom-up, or a combination of both. Let's look at all three variations.

Top-down management
1. Keeps decision-making at the top of the organization.
2. Sets goals, quotas, and direction in the boardroom or at the senior executive level.
3. Has strategic planning meetings or events that include only senior management.
4. Refuses to listen to lower-level employees' ideas, suggestions, or feedback.
5. Coaches and reviews only from the top.
6. Keeps senior-level executives too involved in the hiring process.

7. Has very little, if any, top-down delegation.

Bottom-up management
1. Is the opposite of all of the above.
2. Promotes ownership and buy-in of initiatives and projects from lower-level employees.
3. Wastes fewer resources on activities and programs that don't last.
4. Has more motivated employees.

A combination of both
1. Blends the best approaches, philosophies, and techniques to ensure that employees know what to do, where they are going, and why and how to do it.
2. Ensures that whatever employees are working on is consistent with the direction, focus, mission, vision, core values, and purpose of the organization.

Are you in touch with whether your management style or your organization is top-down or bottom-up? Here's how you can get a fairly accurate picture:
1. Is your corporate direction clear to all employees? If yes, are you sure? How do you know?
2. Is your culture safe for honest bottom-up feedback, or is reality being edited before it gets to you?
3. Do a lot of decisions, projects, and initiatives go bad, sooner or later?
4. Have acquisitions been generally successful over the long term or, after time, was it decided that they were

a mistake?

5. Is morale lower than it should be or than is desirable?
6. Is communication broken anywhere in the organization— top-down, bottom-up, or department-to-department?
7. Is there a "here we go again" culture?
8. Are employees more concerned about the success of their own department than the success of the entire organization?
9. Are you losing some of your better employees?
10. Are sales lagging behind a previous year or years?
11. Is it difficult to hire new, really good people?

Can your organization be both top-down and bottom-up? Yes. And here are some of the benefits:

- Blending of top-down corporate needs with bottom-up accountability
- Combining the creative ideas of lower-level employees with the vision of senior management
- Improving decision-making
- Speeding up problem-solving abilities
- Beating the competition
- Delighting customers

This challenge is well worth it, wouldn't you agree?

Two monologues do not make a dialogue.

—JEFF DALY

CHALLENGE #69: *Being Able to Admit You Didn't Do It, Say It, or Get It Right*

Everyone makes poor decisions from time to time. Everyone exercises poor judgment every now and then too. I haven't met an executive, manager, or business owner who hasn't frequently done something really stupid.

So now that we have that settled, why can't some managers admit to their employees that they made a mistake? Is it ego? Insecurity? Arrogance? It could be all of these and more. The point is that when you have made a mistake, you seldom make it in a vacuum. Sooner or later, everyone knows who was responsible. Admitting mistakes is not a weakness or a demonstration of insecurity, but a sign of confidence, self-knowledge, and inner strength.

Here's the problem. When a manager makes a mistake, he or she can do any of the following things:

- Blame an employee or employees
- Make excuses
- Cover it up
- Go into denial
- Blame their boss
- Claim it's "no big deal"

Each of these actions sends a negative message to your employees. It says, both directly and indirectly, "If you make a mistake, don't take responsibility." These responses can send other messages, too, such as: "Don't try new things. Don't experiment. Don't be creative." People quickly realize that you can't make mistakes if you play it safe. The problem is that in a competitive world, it is very difficult to remain competitive if you are not stretching or testing the unknown.

Playing it safe is an excellent way to ensure that sooner or later, your products or services will hit the scrap pile along with hundreds of other products and services from other companies that also believed it was better to play it safe and avoid failures, mistakes, and errors in judgment than to create and foster a culture that encourages stepping out of your comfort zone and attempting anything, even when its outcome is uncertain.

It is not weakness to admit you were wrong. In fact, it tells your employees that you know you are fallible and that the only way to grow is to stretch with confidence into unfamiliar territory.

It is better to go down in flames trying and growing than to fail quietly while no one notices or cares.

It is definitely challenging to choose and develop your own particular leadership style, behavior patterns, beliefs, and legacy, but this is one of the most significant decisions and actions you will take as an effective leader. All you have to do if you are uncertain is ask yourself a simple question: will my employees follow me, no matter what?

We learn nothing when we succeed.
We only learn when we fail.

—WERNER VON BRAUN

CHAPTER 11

TEAMBUILDING CHALLENGES

One of the topics I am frequently asked to address with my clients is how to get people who come from different areas of the organization to work together more effectively as a team, even though these people also may have different education levels, experience, agendas, time with the organization, and roles. It is not an easy task to get two people to consistently work together effectively, let alone a group of people who may not see each other on a regular basis and must communicate via telephone, memo, or email.

There are a number of issues that must be taken into consideration when orchestrating a group of diverse individuals to work together toward a common goal, objective, or mission.

Some of these are:

- Managing individual creativity
- Managing the individual need for appreciation, recognition, or acceptance
- Dealing with individual ego needs, power struggles, and/or group politics

- Pulling together a group that may have very busy schedules—with travel, different work shifts, vacation time, and time off
- Leading the group toward a common goal rather than a variety of individual ones
- Managing the natural conflicts that will develop as a result of different personality styles interacting
- Keeping the group or team motivated, knowing that motivation is an individual and very personal responsibility
- Knowing what to do with the team when it must disband for whatever reason
- Indoctrinating a new member into the team process after the project is well under way
- Sharing information equally and in a timely manner with all members of the team

Each of these can be difficult to administer. Team leadership requires finesse, tact, skill, patience, courage, a firm hand, good people skills, outstanding persuasion skills, ego control, judgment, effective communication skills, and planning—lots of planning.

I expect to pass through this life but once. If, therefore, there be any kindness I can show, or any good thing I can do for any fellow being, let me do it now, and not defer or neglect it, as I shall not pass this way again.

—WILLIAM PENN

CHALLENGE #70: *Maintaining Effective People Skills*

Several years ago, there was a study done by a major business magazine to determine why managers and executives fail. The conclusion, after evaluating thousands of terminated managers, was that the number one cause of poor management performance wasn't experience, management skills, or ability—it was poor people skills.

People skills. This is such a generic term, and it makes you wonder what people actually mean when they say someone has poor or good people skills. Is it the ability to:

- Motivate?
- Listen?
- Communicate?
- Care?
- Understand?
- Have compassion?
- Be sensitive to others?
- Give people everything they want and need?
- Take adequate time for people?

If you are a manager with poor people skills (however you choose to define them), your organization's or department's performance will be less than stellar. If you have great people skills, you most likely have dedicated, loyal, hard-working, motivated, and effective employees.

So, what's the difference between good and bad people skills? I believe the key lies in sending a clear and consistent message that your employees are important, worthy of respect, valued, and cared about.

CHALLENGE #71: *Mastering the Teambuilding Basics*

Let me give you a few basics about teams before I delve into the challenge of teambuilding in more detail.

1. Any group of two or more people constitutes a team.
2. Every team has unique qualities that contribute to its success or failure.
3. Every team has both internal and external issues and pressures that impact its functioning.
4. Every team must effectively manage diversity in its members.
5. Conflict will be a natural by-product of any team's dynamics.
6. How these conflicts are managed will determine the ultimate success of the team.
7. There are fundamental laws that govern a team's performance and outcomes, just as there are laws that determine individual success.
8. Every team will go through stages of development and decline or renewal while it is an active entity.

Athletes who participate in team sports know the necessity of teamwork. When they lose track of this important quality, and a single member of the group becomes the focal point, the overall results suffer—if not in the short term, then certainly in the long term.

One of the coach's primary functions is to continue to reinforce this team spirit and atmosphere among its members. It is important that each member strive toward his or her full potential without damaging the spirit of the "whole."

If your employees think of teambuilding as a top-down process, and management takes the credit for its creation and nurturing, eventually it will be replaced by another more-or-less-effective fad or process. I do not mean to imply that teambuilding is a fad. But it will be perceived as just another passing tactic of management to improve individual performance and organization profits if it does not become etched into the fiber of the business.

If teambuilding is seen as the concoction of management gurus and philosophers, it will have a short life also, due to the employees' lack of first-hand experience with both the process and function of how teams work. But if it is perceived as an inspiration of the employees, they will take ownership of its necessity, process, and success.

Several elements are involved in how an individual and a team function. I would like to discuss briefly the one I believe is the most critical.

Individuals each have a self-concept that affects their performance, self-worth, and success. This self-image becomes the most critical elements of people's psyche, often determining their further developing attitudes about life, themselves, their roles, and their future. So a team (which is, of course, made up of individuals with their own particular self-concepts) becomes a composite of the accumulated self-issues of the team members. What does this mean in terms of team performance and outcomes?

Every individual performs consistently with their self-image. If a sales person feels they are a $100,000-a-month producer, that's where their monthly sales will range—anywhere from $85,000 to $115,000 a month, usually no better or worse than their average. This average is a composite of their self-worth, self-image, and self-concept. There is no way an individual can achieve consistently greater results than they think they are capable of. Yes, there will be spurts and slumps here and there, but generally their results will fall within this range.

The same holds true for a team. There is a team self-image, self-concept, and self-worth. Their results and approach to opportunities and problems will be consistent with these self-fulfilling team attitudes.

Achieving consistently better results with the individual salesperson requires an internal change in thinking, not changes in territories, prices, products, and quotas. Achieving better results with the team requires the same strategy. The team must feel worthwhile, and the individuals must feel good about the group as a team, their mission, and role.

The job of the team leader and/or manager is to build the self-image of the team. This is no easy task when you consider that the team is made up of multiple "self-images," some positive and some negative.

So, what can you do to manage this diversity?

1. Accurately assess the qualities of each team member in advance.
2. Ask yourself: Is the team's objective too big for this individual's self-concept?
3. Ask yourself: Does this individual function well in a group environment?

4. Accurately describe the role, objectives, challenges, and opportunities to the team.
5. Insist on full ownership in the outcome by each member. Make it a "no-exit" team.
6. Foster an environment of trust and respect before you attempt to tackle a difficult objective.
7. Accept personality, perception, attitude, and philosophy differences.
8. Keep the "team" focus uppermost. There can be no individual stars.
9. Create a safe environment that is free of judgment and criticism.
10. Eliminate hidden agendas.
11. Encourage self-disclosure.
12. Accept conflict as normal in any team process.

Now you know why teambuilding is one of the more exciting challenges!

The purpose of learning is growth, and our minds, unlike our bodies, can continue growing as long as we live.

—MORTIMER ADLER

CHAPTER 12

MEETING CHALLENGES

There are numerous meetings that take place every day in organizations. These can range from informal spur-of-the-moment meetings, weekly staff update meetings, monthly executive briefings, board meetings, and training meetings to strategic planning retreats. There are also meetings with clients, staff, and suppliers, and spontaneous meetings when people say, "Let's take a few minutes and get together to see if we can work this out, solve this, or come up with some creative ideas."

Most meetings generally take too long, cover too little, end without specific plans, objectives, or outcomes, and waste time, money, and resources. Yet I believe that "meeting" is an important business function. Meetings get people together to share information, ideas, problems, activities, solutions, and feelings.

What would you guess is the total number of man-hours spent in meetings in your department or organization in a month? Just multiply the total number of meetings every day for a thirty-day period, by the number of people in those meetings, by the length of time (in minutes), then divide by sixty, and then multiply by twenty. If you can handle a little more, you can also take your average hourly wage (that includes the payroll for executives and managers who probably are not on an hourly wage) and multiply that number by your total number of meeting hours. This exercise might take a few minutes, and don't do it if you are on any kind of heart medication.

My research indicates that most managers and executives spend too much time in meetings and not enough time taking actions or making decisions that will solve the problems that cause the need for more meetings. Actually, my research found that 63 percent of managers said that most of the meetings they attend are redundant, a waste of time, or poorly run.

How does a smart manager turn this around? Read on.

CHALLENGE #72: *Achieving Closure in Meetings*

If you have ever been to a meeting where more of the agenda was left on the table unfinished at the end of a meeting than was accomplished, welcome to one of the most common meeting challenges: getting closure. Why do meetings end without closure on items (for example, problems, issues, or programs) that are put off or pushed forward again and again? Numerous reasons, including the following major ones:

- Too aggressive an agenda
- Not effectively managing discussions, conflict, or the contributions of the participants
- Poor meeting leadership
- People burned-out from too many meetings
- Meeting interruptions
- Lack of overall meeting control
- Participants not given a heads-up in advance on what will be covered
- Poor time management
- Lack of an emotionally safe meeting environment where people can and do share real feelings, opinions, and ideas
- Meeting by egos
- Unresolved personal agendas
- Corporate culture of manipulation, secrecy, or a lack of trust
- People who need to be present are absent

So what's the answer to getting closure on any meeting, whether a three-day strategic planning meeting or a meeting to discuss changing an outdated policy or procedure? Here are a few ideas to consider:

1. Keep meetings on track by limiting or eliminating tangential discussions. Stay focused on the topics at hand.

2. Do not move to a new agenda item until you have closure on the previous topic. Better to resolve one item, even if it takes the entire meeting, than to leave after a lengthy discussion on several topics and then adjourn without conclusions on any of them.

3. Rotate who leads routine meetings. If it is a weekly staff meeting, why not delegate the planning and running of the meeting each week to a different manager?

4. Have a set of meeting rules in advance that everyone is aware of and ensure that everyone adheres to them.

5. Control distractions, side conversations, and interruptions.

6. Don't have meetings during a meal; this wastes too much time.

7. Give people an agenda in advance of the meeting, advising them of what will be covered, the objectives, and what they are expected to contribute.

Wise men talk because they have something to say; fools, because they have to say something.

—PLATO

CHALLENGE #73: *Setting and Following Clear Meeting Objectives*

There are all kinds of meetings held every day in Corporate America:

- Hallway meetings ("Hey, Harry, do you have a minute to talk about this?")
- Weekly or monthly staff or department meetings
- Last-minute meetings caused by an unexpected problem or challenge
- Product-review meetings, employee-review meetings, or training meetings, for example

The purpose of meetings is generally to solve a problem, make a plan, determine a policy, get input, share information, arrive at a decision or direction, or just keep people informed. When meeting objectives are clearly established and communicated, you can generally expect positive, productive outcomes. And just because you determine a set of meeting objectives before a meeting doesn't mean you have to limit the discussion to the planned agenda items—as long as you are adhering to your meeting objectives.

Meetings can be an extremely valuable tool for keeping all employees current with accurate information because they all get the same information at the same time, leaving a smaller likelihood of confusion, misunderstanding, or miscommunication. They are also an excellent way to get consensus on a decision or plan.

But meetings can get derailed when any of the following take place:

1. People who need to be in the meeting are not there.
2. People who don't need to be in the meeting are there.
3. People have to get to their next meeting so they rush though the one they're in.
4. People don't know why they are at this particular meeting.
5. People bring lots of old baggage to any meeting.
6. Discussion topics run wild with no apparent purpose.
7. People vent for reasons having nothing to do with the meeting agenda.

If you have previously determined who should properly be at a particular meeting, and everyone knows the meeting objectives in advance—not necessarily the agenda, but that helps, too—then you have done your homework to prepare for a valuable, purposeful, and productive meeting. All that's left now is to get on with it.

What is the use of a plan if we do not work it?

—JOHN WANAMAKER

CHALLENGE #74: *Conducting Productive Meetings*

What can you do to ensure you are not wasting your employees' time, demotivating them with poor meetings, and contributing to their poor productivity? Here are twenty simple questions to ask yourself in order to conduct more effective meetings. There are others, but if you follow these, you will be well on your way to more productive meetings.

1. Is this meeting necessary? Now? Why?
2. Have you carefully considered who should attend the meeting and why? What will they add or what do they need to take away from it? Do the participants you have selected to attend really need to be there? Or is it that they always have attended this particular meeting and that's the only rationale for their attendance?
3. Have you carefully anticipated possible distractions, obstacles, problems, and responses? Have you planned for them?
4. Who will chair or run the meeting? Why him or her?
5. What is the general theme or purpose of the meeting?
6. Typically, how do the attendees respond or react to your meetings? Why? What can you do to improve their reaction?
7. Do you have a written, clear, specific, and action-focused agenda?
8. Have you let people know the agenda in advance, so they can come prepared to ask questions or contribute intelligently?
9. Do you follow the agenda?

10. Do you encourage opposing viewpoints and ideas?
11. Do you stick to the allotted time?
12. Do you make sure you don't get bogged down and you keep the meeting moving?
13. Do you stay focused in the present?
14. Have you constructively managed the different personalities attending the meeting?
15. Do you make clear, even bold, decisions?
16. Do you get closure on items or establish a specific time to meet again to address tabled issues?
17. Do you hold accountable those people who leave with assigned tasks or activities?
18. Do you leave your ego in the coat closet?
19. Have you validated the participants, whatever their contribution may be?
20. Do you start and end on time?

Well done is better than well said.

—BEN FRANKLIN

CHAPTER 13

COMMUNICATION CHALLENGES

Communication is the movement of information. Effective communication, or the lack of it, stands out head and shoulders above all other challenges as the single biggest problem facing organizations today. Whether the message being communicated is top-down, bottom-up, department-to-department, inside the organization to outside, or outside the organization to inside, the lack of clear communication is costing thousands of organizations their productivity, sales, and profits.

All the clients I have worked with have had some degree of communication problems throughout their organizations. Some have been critical issues that drastically affected their bottom line, while others were nothing more than annoying inconveniences. And there was a lot in between. Regardless of the type of communication challenge you face, I will bet that it is costing you money.

If you can answer six simple questions with accuracy, you are in touch with your organization's communication issues.

If you can't, I suggest you spend some time and energy searching out the answers. It might just improve customer satisfaction, employee performance, profits, and sales.

1. Do you have a communication problem in your organization?
2. If yes, in which direction(s) is it the biggest problem?
3. Why does the problem exist?
4. How long has it been a problem?
5. Who is responsible for the problem?
6. Why hasn't it been solved?

The key to improving communication is reducing misunderstanding and improving clarity. Here are some tried-and-true suggestions for improving communication in your organization:

1. Conduct a confidential employee survey of perceptions, problems, issues, and concerns.
2. Inspect what you expect when it comes to messages that are being sent throughout the organization.
3. Create effective and timely systems of moving information from person to person or department to department.
4. Find the areas where communication seems to be breaking down and develop strategies to improve it.
5. Be more concerned with what the message is rather than its source.
6. Foster a culture that encourages the honest sharing of information.
7. Don't shoot the messenger who brings bad news.

8. Conduct regular staff meetings and encourage a discussion of reality.

In a nutshell:
1. Assume nothing.
2. Inspect everything.
3. Find the source of the problem (person, policy, or procedure).
4. Determine what the problem is costing you directly and indirectly.
5. If it is a recurring problem, ask yourself why.
6. Get closer to the problem.
7. Ask the people who are closest to the problem what it is and why they think it exists or persists.
8. Encourage upward feedback of accurate information.
9. If you are a senior person in the organization, take full responsibility for the problem.

Don't forget until too late that the business of life is not business, but living.

—B.C. FORBES

CHALLENGE #75: *Sending Consistent Top-Down Messages*

One of the most significant issues that affects organizational productivity is the lack of consistency between top-down messages, communication, expectations, corporate culture, and bottom-up reality. Often employees hear different messages, depending on who is the source of the message. The message could, for example, be emanating from the president, their managers, or some department head. Although this is a considerable problem on an internal basis, it becomes increasingly important when communicating with customers, vendors, and prospective customers.

Let me give you a recent example. A manager told an employee that a new product was to be presented to a new customer in a meeting the following week. When the salesperson called production and shipping to determine when she would receive a sample of the product for her presentation, a manufacturing manager (in the department that produced that product) told her that he didn't know where she got the information that this new product would be available by the following week. In fact, it wasn't going to be available for thirty to sixty days. After calling her manager back to get clarification, her manager said: "That manager in manufacturing doesn't know what he is talking about. The product is available now." I could go on and on with the ripple effect of this situation, but I am sure you see the root of the problem here.

This salesperson is getting mixed messages from two senior managers. One of them has to be wrong. What is she to do regarding the appointment with this customer?

Mixed and conflicting messages like this occur on a regular basis in your organization, I will guarantee it. There is a tremendous cost—both direct and indirect—as a result of these miscommunications.

- What is the cause of these mixed messages?
- Who is responsible for them?
- Why do they persist?

Yes, these are difficult questions. But the real question is: how can you avoid these often simple misinterpretations of policy, procedure, philosophy, or strategy? Here are some questions you can ask yourself:

1. Are there certain people or departments where this problem is more prevalent?
2. Is there a history of these types of problems in your organization?
3. Are there certain times of the year, month, or week when these occur more frequently?
4. Is the problem getting worse?
5. As a manager, are you aware that these problems are even happening?
6. Do you know the cost of these problems in terms of customer satisfaction, profits, sales, or morale?

Act decidedly and take the consequences. No good is ever done by hesitation.

—THOMAS HUXLEY

CHALLENGE #76: *Seeing Disagreement as Valuable*

One of the common errors poor managers make today is to shoot the messenger who brings bad news. Their attitude is often:

1. You are not a team player.
2. You are always negative.
3. You are always complaining.
4. You are never happy.
5. You are a pain in the—.

I will agree that some employees fit one or all of the above characterizations, but when you have an employee bring you bad news, do you:

- Thank them?
- Criticize them?
- Ignore them?
- Berate them?
- Listen to them?
- Encourage them to tell you more?

The point is: the closer you are to reality (either with a situation inside the organization or outside with customers or suppliers), the better the decisions you can make. And that will tend to ensure your success and organization performance. Shooting the messenger is a great way to ensure you are totally out of touch with the conditions, perceptions, attitudes, problems, and challenges that are present in your department or organization as a whole.

Let me repeat: if all you ever hear is good news and never the bad news, you are contributing to your ultimate failure as a manager and possibly as an organization. The key to better managing conflict is not to try to eliminate it, but to ensure that trust and respect are present in all working relationships and that these are used as the foundation for exchanging ideas, suggestions, information, and even disagreement. Here are a few ideas to consider the next time one of your employees brings you bad news or you perceive them as being disagreeable or disloyal.

1. Create and foster a culture that encourages or even rewards truthful bad news.
2. Don't just listen to the people who believe what you believe.
3. Don't berate or criticize employees who bring you less than ideal news.
4. Listen to employees who bring bad news or criticism, and ask for additional information on the message they bring.
5. Do something with the information, and let the person know what you did.
6. Empower people to be on the lookout for bad news.
7. Put a system in place that permits all news—good and bad—to get to the top.
8. Tell your employees you want it all: the good, the bad, and the ugly.

Know how to listen, and you will profit even from those who talk badly.

—Plutarch

CHALLENGE #77: *Validating Employees*

What is a "validator"? It is a person who makes people feel good about themselves, contributes to the improvement of their self-esteem, listens to them, and is interested in their opinions and feedback. Validators don't put other people down, insult them in public, disregard their opinions, or let their own egos try to control other people; they are not emotionally manipulative and don't negate other people's feelings.

Unfortunately, *in*validators are everywhere: in the home, the classroom, the boardroom, and on the golf course. What's an invalidator? The complete opposite of a validator.

How do you know whether you are a validator? Here are a few clues:

1. You let people speak without interrupting them.
2. You listen to people.
3. You respect other people's feelings.
4. You care about the needs of others.
5. You say "Do you" (rather than "Don't you") when asking a question.
6. You treat your employees as your primary resource.
7. You avoid judgmental remarks that begin with: "You should... you never... you always... you don't... you owe me...."
8. You refrain from putting guilt trips on people with comments such as: "If you really cared about this company you would...." "Why can't you be more like...?"

There are a lot more, but I am sure you can now identify whether you are a validator or if you have one working for you. Here are a few things you can do if you feel you are an invalidator and need to improve the way you interact with your employees.

1. Change your behavior. This can take a great deal of personal awareness, commitment, desire, time, effort, and the willingness to accept full responsibility for your actions and behaviors.

2. Get yourself into some career counseling.

3. Record your conversations with others and play them back to yourself later, looking for ways you may have invalidated or validated others.

4. Read my book, *Nit-Pickers, Naggers, and Tyrants*.

5. Share the concept of validation with your employees, and ask them to be honest and tell you if you are a validator. You can develop a simple survey for this. If you have to do this anonymously, you don't even need the survey; you already know their answers.

6. Give your employees a signal they can use every time you invalidate them. For example, whenever you interrupt them, they can whistle. Every time you compliment, they nod their head. I guarantee it won't take long for you to develop an awareness about whether you are a validator or invalidator.

7. Ask a third party (maybe your assistant or a peer) to act as an observer. If you invalidate another person, whether in a meeting or in a small-group discussion, the observer brings this to your attention.

8. Develop some rules of behavior for yourself and your employees as to how people will treat each other.

9. Accept the simple truth that everything in life is perceptual. Even though you might think you are making a validating statement or exhibiting validating behavior, it may not always be interpreted as you intended or thought it would be.

Being a validator yourself—and being around validators—is good for the energy level of your employees, their confidence, self-esteem, and ultimate performance. Does it get better than that?

CHALLENGE #78: *Encouraging and Listening to Bottom-Up Feedback*

The view at the lower echelons of your organization is usually more accurate than the view at the top of the corporate ladder in terms of the reality of what is going on in your organization as well as with your customers and suppliers. Yes, managers and executives often see the bigger picture, but believe me, your ultimate success is in the details and in their implementation. And I will guarantee that your employees know more than many of their managers about how to fix things, solve problems, take advantage of opportunities, and make decisions that impact their performance.

Here's the problem: if you don't have a systematic way of getting this reality higher up the organizational ladder, your company will make bad decisions and judgments. If you are not receptive to honest, bottom-up feedback for any reason, then you will be operating in a dangerous and risky vacuum.

The challenge for managers is to accept bottom-up feedback, information, communication, ideas, reality, and solutions as valuable and worthwhile. Managers alone do not have all the solutions and ideas, nor are they the only ones with the ability to make sound decisions that will benefit their organizations.

One of the healthiest behaviors you can have as a manager is to encourage, reward, support—even compensate—employees who bring you ideas, feedback, and opinions. I know that it can often be hard to accept that you are not perfect, that you make mistakes and don't always know what is best, but let's get real. Can you remember years back, before you were a manager or executive? Didn't you have great ideas, input, or solutions? And how did you feel if they were ignored, squashed, or, even worse, someone else like your boss or another department head took the credit for them?

Learn to trust, respect, and validate your employees by encouraging and then listening with an open mind to their contributions. What have you got to lose?

CHALLENGE #79: *Listening Even When You Disagree*

It's a big enough challenge for some managers and leaders to be willing to really listen to their rank-and-file employees, but it's altogether more challenging to listen when you disagree with what they are telling you. Despite this, keep in mind that you have a much better chance at dealing with the reality of your department or company if:

1. Your corporate culture is open and receptive.
2. You validate employees' ideas and suggestions.
3. You encourage the upward flow of honest information.
4. You reward honesty and quality rather than negative employee traits.
5. Employees believe you really want the truth or the information they have to give you.

Here are a few ideas to help you succeed in listening to "the bad news" or whatever doesn't match your own thinking or expectations:

1. Keep your ego out of the way of communication.
2. Set aside your own prejudices, opinions, values, judgments, and expectations.
3. Recognize that life is a perceptual experience. Whatever perceptions (true or false) your employees have, these perceptions are true for them.
4. Play with the idea that no one is ever really wrong. They just need more information to come to a different conclusion. This could be the employee—or it could be you.

5. Learn to accept others for who they are, what they think, how they feel, and what they believe.
6. Encourage your employees not to edit what they tell you.
7. Believe that your employees have your organization's best interests at heart.
8. Don't rely on a single source in your organization for accurate information.
9. Be consistent in your behavior, regardless of how difficult it might be at certain times.
10. Pay close attention to rumors, the grapevine, and hearsay—they communicate information you might not get otherwise.

CHALLENGE #80: *Understanding the Importance of Perception*

One of the best indicators of someone who is happy, successful, and living with their world in a harmonious way is how clearly they are in touch with reality—not "their reality," but *reality*. It is not our interpretation of it. Yet so many people believe that their truth (their *perceptions* of the truth) should be everyone's truth. Since perceptions are such a critical part of a person's performance, at the risk of being redundant let me repeat: between one person's truth and another's, there is no right or wrong; there are only differences.

People don't "yes" or "rubber stamp" us because everyone sees life differently. Everyone looks through their own set of personal filters. As we survey our relationships with employees, customers, friends, and relatives, we can notice degrees of conflict everywhere—in beliefs, actions, and due to unrealized expectations.

I have observed a great deal of human behavior over the past forty years in the marketplace. I truly believe that if we are to live with balance, peace, and harmony, we must look squarely at how we perceive and interpret life and how we act upon what we see.

Each of us brings unique knowledge and experience to every relationship and situation. All of us are right in our own minds. "Our truth" is what works for us. But truth—with a capital T—is no respecter of opinions, fads, arrogance, or ignorance. We cannot manipulate Truth to fit our own sense of values or beliefs.

In my early speaking career, I hadn't learned yet that everyone doesn't have to agree with me. It was not my role or responsibility to change their minds. We are all at different stages of personal and professional development. This doesn't make some right or others wrong.

Take a look at some of the people or circumstances that contribute to your stress or frustration—whether at work, home, or anywhere else in your life. What is it about these people or situations that trigger your anxiety, fear, or whatever emotion you feel when you interact with these stressors? Where do your expectations come from? Why do people disappoint you? Why does life reward or punish you?

Answering these challenging questions, congratulating yourself on your self-awareness, and implementing any change that would make you a better manager, a better leader, or a better person, will be well worth the effort.

The first ingredient in communication is truth; the next, good sense; the third, good humor, and the fourth, wit.

—SIR WILLIAM TEMPLE

CHALLENGE #81: *Managing Your Expectations*

Expectations—unrealized expectations—of other people's behavior can cause us more stress and grief than just about anything else. Why is this? Because the execution of all behavior by others is in their hands, not yours.

Managing your expectations means understanding that other people are all doing the best they can, at any given moment, with what they have learned thus far. We are all learning every day, either by accident, design, or on purpose, but we are all learning what life wants us to learn now. Keep in mind that most other people are not setting out deliberately to disappoint you, upset you, or make you miserable.

Managing expectations also requires that we learn to accept others as they grow through the individual lessons that life has thrown in their path. They may not always act as we would or think they should, but guess what? That's OK.

Life just happens. I believe in setting goals, planning, and spending time trying to figure out how to create a better future. The problem is: life can change in a heartbeat. I will guarantee for at least one person who is reading this book—yes, even you—that your life has not turned out, in every way, the way you planned it or thought it would.

A year ago, I never thought I would be writing this book. If you would have told me when I was twenty-five years old, that by age sixty-five, I would have written more than sixty books, spoken in more than twenty countries, and spoken to more than a million people, my response would have been "You must be talking about someone else."

You and I have done things we never planned to, both positive and negative, and we have not yet done some things that we have planned to, thought about, or worked toward, for many years. Expectations or outcomes are not guaranteed but always in a state of uncertainty.

LET'S SUMMARIZE

No matter what else you do as a manager, there are three things that can guarantee increased sales, profits, and improved employee performance and effectiveness. They are focus, clear direction, and effective communication. Yes, there are other areas you need to pay close attention to, as we have discussed in the preceding pages, but my guess is that most of them will fall directly or indirectly under these three. Let's review each of them briefly.

Focus
There is a psychological concept that basically says: what you tend to focus on—in your life, business, career, or relationships—tends to increase. In other words, if your concentration and awareness are always on what is wrong or negative, guess what? It will continue to be wrong and negative. As a manager, if your focus is on what is not working somewhere in your organization, then it will be difficult to change it for the better. This does not mean that you should stick your

head in the sand and ignore it or act like it doesn't exist. It means, "Keep your eye on the doughnut and not on the hole" as you deal with the situation.

There is a great old saying attributed to Albert Einstein: "Insanity is doing the same thing over and over and expecting different results." OK, so business is coming back slowly for some of you. For others it may still be performing poorly. Whatever. I ask you, where is your focus and the focus of your employees? On what you do well, what you do right, and your successes? Or on everything that is wrong?

Clear direction

Seeing the future clearly is always a challenge—to everyone, of course, not just managers and leaders. In many cases, it is downright impossible. The problem is, you still have to grow your business and make money today as well as tomorrow, and do it while taking a lot of risks that you can't guarantee will pay off in the long run. From your perspective as a manager, this poses a problem that can cause stress, frustration, fear, and insecurity. Imagine what it is doing to your employees who do not have the vantage point or ability to see past their next assignment.

A few of the common statements and questions I hear from employees during my interviews in preparation for a custom in-house training assignment is: "Who are we, where are we going, how are we going to get there, or how do I fit in to the future of this organization?" Imagine for a minute that you are such an employee and you are not privy to some senior-level information, goals, or strategies. What can you do? You can do your job—that's it—with no creativity, no imagination, no innovation, and no ownership in the ultimate outcome. Now, what if every employee had this attitude? You guessed it: you get the labor of their hands, but not their hearts. It's tough to grow and compete if this is your culture or corporate mindset.

Communication

The movement of information in any organization is top-down, bottom-up, or department-to-department. You would be surprised at how much redundancy takes place in many organizations because the primary method of communication is:

1. You have to be in the right place at the right time.
2. You have to be high enough on the food chain.
3. You have to be in the "in group."
4. You have to fight for every scrap of information that you need to do your job right or better.

Again I ask you: how well can employees do their jobs if they do not have the information they need to be effective?

I don't care what else you accomplish this year. If you can effectively address these three issues, you will be amazed at how much more profitable and competitive you can be in the marketplace.

Again, "Insanity is doing the same thing over and over and expecting different results." I am amazed at how frequently this quote has applied to me and various areas of my life. How about you? Does it apply to any area of your business today? A department? Policy? Procedure? You and your attitudes, expectations, or behaviors?

To combat this habit of repeating mistakes in judgment, decisions, or actions, I have developed the following four questions that I ask myself every month, quarter, and year. I often share these questions with my audiences to get them thinking.

The four questions are:

1. What are you doing in your life, career, or business that is working? Why is it working?
2. What are you doing in these same areas that is not working? Why isn't it working?
3. What did you formerly do in these areas that used to work—that you have stopped doing? When and why did you stop doing these things?
4. What should you begin doing in these areas that you have not done in the past?

Answering these four critical questions can keep you traveling in the right direction in all areas of your business, career, and life, if you will ask them often enough and pay close attention to the answers you get.

The purpose of this exercise is to ensure that you are:

1. Focusing on the right things in the right way.
2. Letting go of old stuff that isn't working.
3. Re-evaluating your career, business, and life from a past as well as a future orientation.
4. Stretching yourself into new areas of development.

5. Experimenting with new strategies, attitudes, philosophies, feelings, and skills.
6. Reinventing yourself each year.
7. Staying ahead of the curve of relentless change.

Many people are stuck in old ways of thinking, doing, and believing that just are not working for them anymore. Many managers, executives, and business owners are bogged down in products, policies, and approaches that are just not working—and may never work—but they hold on to them for dear life, regardless. Why? Fear? Comfort? Indecision? Arrogance? Ignorance? Ego? Politics? It could be any or all of these or other reasons.

Are you holding on to something that you need to let go of? For example:

- A product that has outlived its purpose or usefulness
- An unproductive or negative employee that is sabotaging the productivity of a department or the organization
- A policy that should have been changed months or years ago
- An attitude or prejudice that is getting in the way of your personal success
- A management style that is counterproductive
- A procedure that is redundant or counterproductive
- A habit that is keeping you or your organization from improved effectiveness

Why not spend some time on these final points to see if you can uncover any areas that need modification or abandonment?

If you feel really daring, why not show these points to some of your employees or direct reports for their responses, too?

The only limit to our realization of tomorrow will be our doubts of today; Let us move forward with strong and active faith.

—FRANKLIN D. ROOSEVELT

READY TO RATE YOURSELF AS A MANAGER?

Your results as a manager are evident by the achievements you have accomplished, as well as the challenges, failures, and goals that were, for whatever reason, not realized. One of the behaviors I have been advocating for managers for many years is the careful and routine evaluation of the areas where they have made progress and where they have not.

There are many benefits to this type of activity. Yet many managers are too busy, too stressed, or just unwilling to take the time to conduct a thorough self-evaluation of their strengths, weaknesses, failures, or self-development needs.

For many years, I have been sharing ideas, concepts, and techniques with managers around the world on how best to improve organizational performance and employee productivity. It still amazes me, however, how few of these individuals have the courage or interest to look periodically in the mirror with an eye toward getting better. As I've said throughout these chapters: if you have a problem in your organization, look up the ladder and not down for its cause. If you are not willing to take full responsibility for the outcomes, behaviors, attitudes, or failures in your organization, then you might want to consider a job as a Wal-Mart greeter.

One easy way to accomplish this activity is with my 3/3/3 Quarterly Review Process (see Challenge #38). This simple device is used by managers as well as employees, for both a top-down and bottom-up evaluation of skill and attitude development needs. Hundreds of organizations and thousands of employees and managers are currently using the

3/3/3 Quarterly Review Process.

It really doesn't matter what device, system, or strategy you use to determine your progress or development as a manager, executive, or business owner. What does matter is that you use something that has integrity, reality, honesty, and timeliness. You can't just sit in a limbo state of performance. If you are not getting better as a manager, you are likely getting worse. If you are getting better, it is important to determine if you are improving in the right areas and in the right ways.

Show me a manager or executive who is unwilling to accept honest bottom-up feedback from employees, customers, or the marketplace, and I will show you a manager who is most likely sabotaging the performance and success of his or her organization.

If you are a new manager, it is vital that you develop the right attitudes and approaches to developing yourself and your employees. Yes, it takes time, commitment, money, and energy to get better. But in the long run, it is far better to improve your people, management, and leadership skills than to assume that yesterday's knowledge, approaches, and philosophy are still relevant today. The times they are a-changing, folks—keep up or fall behind!

---

* If you would like a copy to evaluate for potential use in your organization, I will give you a 50 percent discount on the first copy (regularly $15.00). To receive your evaluation copy, just go to my website (www.timconnor.com) and order the 3/3/3. Click on the Learning Materials/Resources link, then click on Books & CDs (the category is Assessments), and be sure to write 50-percent-off discount when you get to the comments section. The shopping cart will not compute the discount. Not to worry. We process all our website credit card orders in our office manually, so we will give you your earned discount before charging your credit card.

If I fail, it will be for lack of ability and not of purpose.

—ABRAHAM LINCOLN

IT'S YOUR TURN

In this section, I recommend that you review each of the challenges discussed in each chapter and create a list of those that apply to you frequently or from time to time. Then develop a list of actions you plan to take to transform your behavior and management style.

CHALLENGES I NEED TO FACE

Challenge #1:

_____

_____

Actions I plan to take:

_____

_____

_____

_____

Challenge #2:

_____

_____

Actions I plan to take:

_____

_____

_____

_____

Challenge #3:

_____

_____

Actions I plan to take:

_____

_____

_____

Challenge #4:

_____

_____

Actions I plan to take:

_____

_____

_____

_____

Challenge #5:

_____

_____

Actions I plan to take:

_____

_____

_____

_____

Challenge #6:

_____

_____

Actions I plan to take:

_____

_____

_____

Challenge #7:

_____

_____

Actions I plan to take:

_____

_____

_____

_____

Challenge #8:

_____

_____

Actions I plan to take:

_____

_____

_____

_____

Challenge #9:

_____

_____

Actions I plan to take:

_____

_____

_____

Challenge #10:

_____

_____

Actions I plan to take:

_____

_____

_____

_____

Challenge #11:

_____

_____

Actions I plan to take:

_____

_____

_____

_____

Challenge #12:

_____

_____

Actions I plan to take:

_____

_____

_____

Challenge #13:

_____

_____

Actions I plan to take:

_____

_____

_____

_____

Never mistake motion for action.

—ERNEST HEMINGWAY

MANAGEMENT QUIZ ANSWERS

Keep in mind that the answers to several of the questions are subjective. In many cases, there is no right or wrong answer, only a best or better answer. With this in mind, let's see how well you did.

1. B. Public
2. A. True
3. A. True
4. A. Private
5. A. True
6. A. Top-down
7. E. All of the above
8. B. Reality
9. A. True
10. E. All of the above
11. B. False
12. B. False
13. A. Beneath your standards

14. B. False
15. A. Direction
16. E. All of the above
17. B. False
18. C. Can be both—and it depends
19. A. True
20. B. False
21. B. False
22. B. Expect
23. A. True
24. B. Reward
25. B. False
26. B. False
27. B. Is a sign of management weakness, sending the wrong message to other employees
28. A. Change or modify behavior
29. A. Skills
30. A. Responsibility and authority
31. B. False
32. A. True
33. B. A statement of direction, purpose, meaning
34. A. Who you are, who your customers are, how you serve them, and the business you are in.
35. C. It depends
36. C. The first three: It makes them feel important; it builds trust and respect; they want to feel they belong to something bigger than themselves.
37. A. True
38. B. False

39. B. False
40. A. True
41. B. Diminish their performance
42. A. True
43. E. All of the above
44. B. False
45. A. True
46. A. True
47. A. True
48. A. True
49. A. Give the credit and take the responsibility
50. B. False

SCORING

50 correct answers: You should be giving the test.

45–49 correct answers: You understand the basics of effective management.

40–44 correct answers: There is hope for you yet.

35–39 correct answers: With luck, you may make it as a manager.

30–34 correct answers: You have a lot to learn. Better get started.

30 or fewer correct answers: You need help big-time—call me today!

©2002, Tim Connor, Management Quiz

RECOMMENDED READING

7 Secrets of Exceptional Leadership—Christopher J. Hegarty and Philip B. Nelson

American Renaissance—Marvin Cetron and Owen Davies

Becoming a Leader—Myles Munroe

Bringing Out the Best in People—Alan Loy McGinnis

Good to Great—Jim Collins

If Aristotle Ran General Motors—Thomas V. Morris

If It Ain't Broke...Break It!—Robert J. Kriegel and Louis Patler

Integrity—Henry Cloud

Leadership A to Z—James O'Toole

Machiavelli on Modern Leadership—Michael A. Ledeen

Managing for Results—Peter F. Drucker

Managing from the Heart—Hyler Bracey, Jack Rosenblum, Aubrey Sanford, and Roy Trueblood

Maslow on Management—Abraham H. Maslow

Motivation and Personality—Abraham H. Maslow

Nasty People—Jay Carter

Reengineering the Corporation—James Hammer and Michael Champy

---

Optimism is the faith that leads to achievement. Nothing can be done without hope or confidence.

—HELEN KELLER

Tim Connor's books, manuals, and CDs are available on his website: www.timconnor.com.

Please send me the following **career and personal development materials:**

___ *81 Management Challenges*—Book—($24.95)

___ *25 Management Principles*—CD Set—($49.00)

___ *The Ancient Scrolls: A Parable*—Book—($15.00)

___ *Beat the Competition NOW*—CD Series—($95.00)

___ *25 Sales Principles*—CD Set—($49.00)

___ *25 Success Principles*—CD Set—($49.00)

___ *The Last Goodbye*—Book—($15.00)

___ *That's Life! 41 Life Challenges and How to Handle Them*—Book—($15.00)

___ *The Sales Handbook*—Book—($15.00)

___ *Soft Sell*—Book—($19.95)

___ *Your First Year in Sales*—Book—($19.95)

___ *How to Sell More in Less Time*—Book—($15.00)

___ *Soft Sell*—CD Set—($49.00)

___ *25 Motivation Principles*—CD Set—($49.00)

TOTAL ORDER: $_____ (PLEASE ADD $5.00 FOR S&H)

Name: _____

Address: _____

_____

_____

City: _____ State:_____

Zip: _____ Tel: _____

Email: _____

○ Enclosed is my check/money order
○ Charge my Visa/MC/AmEx:
  No: _____
  Exp Date: _____

All materials are available for a quantity discount.
Phone Orders: 704-895-1230 • Fax Orders: 704-895-1231
Email Orders: tim@timconnor.com
Mail Orders: Box 397, Davidson, NC 28036
Website: www.timconnor.com

HIRE TIM

To hire Tim Connor for an upcoming meeting or convention, to discuss his custom in-house training programs on management or sales, to discuss using him to facilitate a strategic planning event, or to participate in his Career and Life Coaching Program, contact him at:

Connor Resource Group, Inc.
Box 397
Davidson, NC 28036
(Voice) 704-895-1230
(Fax) 704-895-1231
tim@timconnor.com (Email)
www.timconnor.com

INDEX

Tim Connor, CSP, is the president and CEO of Connor Resource Group, Inc., and Peak Performance Institute. He has been a full-time professional speaker, trainer, coach, consultant, and bestselling author for thirty-five years. Since 1973 he has given more than four thousand presentations in twenty-one countries around the world to a wide variety of audiences.

Each year, more than 85 percent of his presentations are return engagements for previous clients on such topics as peak performance management, effective leadership, customer-focused sales strategies, personal motivation, value-driven customer service, and building positive business and personal relationships.

Every year he also facilitates a number of strategic planning events and meetings for many of his clients, and he presents several public boot camps. He is a results-oriented business coach and consultant working with a select few clients each year to help them improve their individual and organizational performance.

Tim has been a member of the National Speakers Association for more than twenty-five years, and he is one of only four hundred certified speaking professionals (CSP) in the world, a designation bestowed by the National Speakers Association since 1980.

He is the bestselling author of over sixty books, including the international bestsellers *Soft Sell*, *The Ancient Scrolls*, and *Your First Year in Sales*.

Tim's clients range from companies with five million dollars a year in sales to those with more than fifty billion dollars in sales. They come from a wide variety of industries including food manufacturing and distribution, housing and construction, financial services, technology and communication, manufacturing, and personal and professional services.

His presentations are filled with insightful and contemporary ideas and are presented in a riveting and entertaining style.

To discuss hiring Connor for your organization,
contact him at:
Phone: 704-895-1230
Fax: 704-895-1231
Email: tim@timconnor.com
Website: www.timconnor.com